Helping Children to Improve their Communication Skills

by the same author

Helping Children to Cope with Change, Stress and Anxiety
A Photocopiable Activities Book
Deborah M. Plummer
Illustrations by Alice Harper
ISBN 978 1 84310 960 0

Helping Children to Build Self-Esteem
A Photocopiable Activities Book
2nd Edition
Deborah M. Plummer
Illustrated by Alice Harper
ISBN 978 1 84310 488 9

Helping Adolescents and Adults to Build Self-Esteem
A Photocopiable Resource Book
Deborah M. Plummer
ISBN 978 1 84310 185 7

Social Skills Games for Children
Deborah M. Plummer
Foreword by Professor Jannet Wright
Illustrated by Jane Serrurier
ISBN 978 1 84310 617 3

Anger Management Games for Children
Deborah M. Plummer
Illustrated by Jane Serrurier
ISBN 978 1 84310 628 9

Self-Esteem Games for Children
Deborah M. Plummer
Illustrated by Jane Serrurier
ISBN 978 1 84310 424 7

The Adventures of the Little Tin Tortoise
A Self-Esteem Story with Activities for Teachers, Parents and Carers
Deborah M. Plummer
ISBN 978 1 84310 406 3

Using Interactive Imagework with Children
Walking on the Magic Mountain
Deborah M. Plummer
ISBN 978 1 85302 671 3

Helping Children to Improve their Communication Skills

Therapeutic Activities for Teachers, Parents and Therapists

Deborah M. Plummer

Illustrations by Alice Harper

Jessica Kingsley *Publishers*
London and Philadelphia

MW

First published in 2011
by Jessica Kingsley Publishers
116 Pentonville Road
London N1 9JB, UK
and
400 Market Street, Suite 400
Philadelphia, PA 19106, USA

www.jkp.com

Library of Congress Cataloging in Publication Data
Plummer, Deborah.
Helping children to improve their communication skills : therapeutic activities for teachers, parents, and therapists / Deborah M. Plummer ; illustrated by Alice Harper.
p. ; cm.
ISBN 978-1-84310-959-4 (alk. paper)
1. Speech therapy for children. I. Title.
[DNLM: 1. Child. 2. Language Disorders--rehabilitation. 3. Play Therapy. WL 340.2]
RJ496.S7P58 2011
618.92'85506--dc22
2010033885

British Library Cataloguing in Publication Data
A CIP catalogue record for this book is available from the British Library

ISBN 978 1 84310 959 4

Printed and bound in Great Britain by
MPG Books Group

7/8/11

Dedication

For George – an inspired and inspirational communicator.
Without his invaluable support
this book would never have been written.

Contents

Acknowledgements

During my years as a speech and language therapist I have collected many different games and activities from various sources. Some of them have been passed on to me by colleagues in teaching and therapy professions or by children in therapy groups; some came from books; many are adaptations of games I remember playing as a child; some are based on ideas presented on various professional training courses. So, once again, I would like to say a big thank you to everyone who has shared their favourite activities with me over the years and to all the children who have tried these out and who inspired so many of the adapted versions.

My thanks also to Alison Tempest, speech and language therapist and lecturer at De Montfort University, for her insights and encouragement and to Jane Serrurier, teacher and play therapist, for giving her time to numerous discussions about creativity and emotional well-being and for her guidance on adapting activities for different settings.

Note: The pronouns 'he' and 'she' have been used alternately throughout the book to refer to a child of either gender.

Part One

Theoretical and Practical Background

Chapter 1

Introduction: Developing a Therapeutic Imagination

Communication is such a complex process that it is a wonder how any of us manage to develop the necessary abilities and skills required for successful social interaction. Even when such abilities and skills are in place, their effectiveness can so easily be disrupted by tiredness, illness, stress, or periods of heightened self-awareness and fluctuating self-esteem. This book offers a collection of ideas for games and activities to help *all* children develop their communication competence and thereby strengthen their social and emotional well-being and resilience. It is also a celebration of the skills and resilience that children develop in order to fulfil their communication potential. It is an acknowledgement of the power of language and the delight of words, of the wonderful instrument of communication that is our voice, the intricacies of muscle movement and coordination required for speech, the subtleties of facial expression and body movements involved in conveying complex messages to others. The ideas can be used in a variety of settings – for example, in the classroom or at home or as part of a general social skills group. However, for convenience and consistency, and because the needs of children with specific speech, language and communication difficulties are necessarily greater with regard to support, I have referred to 'therapist' and the therapeutic environment throughout Part One. Where a child has an identified communication disorder, the involvement of a speech and language therapist is recommended in order for appropriate assessment to take place and for the structuring of the activities in a way that is suitable for specific needs. The general principles referred to for supporting communication well-being and resilience are relevant for all of us, of course, whether we are parents who are concerned about our own children or practitioners working with children in teaching or therapeutic environments.

The impetus for the book arose from conversations with my colleagues (lecturers and therapists in practice) who are involved in training and supervising speech and language therapy students. We have all watched students engage with children in innovative and fun activities that are clearly effective in helping to teach or reinforce appropriate use of skills. However, it is surprisingly easy for even the most innovative of ideas to lose some of their potential value because of the way in which they are delivered. Conversely, basic materials, often gathered from the immediate environment, which are used creatively, can be extremely effective. My colleagues and I joked about the possible title for this book: should it be 'Beyond the Beanbag' (which later became a chapter heading), or perhaps 'How to Survive without Minimal Pairs Cards'? But, of course, the point is that it is not the equipment that has potential to limit our therapeutic effectiveness, it is our own *therapeutic imagination* – the ability to 'imagine' what it might be like physically, emotionally and cognitively to be the child or adult with whom we are working; to use that ability to monitor and shape our interactions, and to think creatively and imaginatively about how we design and deliver our support.

Although therapy with children who have speech, language and communication needs (SLCN) is always child-centred and is increasingly based on working as part of integrated teams and within a collaborative framework, the need for evidence-based practice and recording of outcomes means that it can be a scary experience for students on placement to step beyond the safety of structured programmes of intervention and to utilise their creative talents. I would argue that it can often be equally as scary for the parents and carers who are encouraged to continue the therapy process at home, and is also often a challenge for more experienced therapists who find themselves devising programmes for others to carry out.

We also need to be aware that integrated working calls for therapy aims to be met in creative ways within curriculum activities. The themes and topics covered within the classroom should inform our therapy, as should the daily activities and interests of the child at home.

So, although this book offers a collection of ideas for supporting children who have SLCN, it is not a recipe book for therapy in the way that some old-fashioned cookery books gave very precise and detailed instructions and exact proportions of ingredients. Such books had the unfortunate potential to deskill completely those of us who, like me, were unsure of our own inventive abilities when it came to anything beyond a basic meal!

Instead, as with some of the more current cookery books which might refer to a 'slug' of olive oil, a 'dollop' of honey or a 'dribble' of vinegar, I would encourage you to view the concocting of sessions for each child and group of children as involving a large degree of creativity rather than being a precise science. Play is the natural medium of learning for children, and is the way in which they tend to express their feelings (Dwivedi 1993). I hope that the ideas presented here will encourage you to have the confidence to create and recreate each session that you do and to have fun with therapy. Treat every session as unique and you will inject a dollop of therapeutic imagination that will undoubtedly engage and motivate the children with whom you work.

My aim throughout the book is to emphasise the importance of helping children to develop *communication well-being* (see Chapter 2). It is now recognised that there is a need to centre our understanding of children's speech, language and communication difficulties and needs on an understanding of the communication process as being pivotal to personal and social well-being, and that we should therefore give just as much or even more time to consideration of the wider impact of our work as we do to facilitating the learning of specific skills. The focus of Part One of this book is therefore firmly centred on methods of optimising the emotional environment for learning.

The activity ideas are based on a framework that distinguishes between three different layers of therapeutic effects, rather than one that highlights particular types of communication impairment or specific needs. I have not, for example, categorised any of the activities according to whether or not they would be useful for working with children with dyspraxia or voice or fluency difficulties, or children with autism and so on. This is because every child is unique in the pattern of his strengths and difficulties almost regardless of the type of com-munication impairment.

The framework that I propose below is intended as a way of emphasising the multilayered effect that participating in different therapy activities can have.

Foundation elements, core abilities and specific skills

There have been many studies indicating that speech and language therapy inter-ventions have effects beyond the improvement of speech or language skills per se. For example, studies have indicated improvements in interpersonal relationships, play, use of coping strategies and reduction in parental stress (Robertson and Weismer 1999) and in self-confidence, enthusiasm for learning and a reduction in displays of frustration (Boyle *et al.* 2009)

When we help children to build communication skills, we are potentially hav-ing a profound effect on their long-term social, emotional, physical and cognitive well-being, perhaps more so than any research will ever be able to demonstrate. In other words, while helping children to develop and improve their speech and language abilities and skills, we are also inevitably helping them to 'become themselves'. This means that we can find ourselves working at more than one level simultaneously – for example, enhancing *core abilities* such as effective listening and observation in order to facilitate *specific skills* such as phoneme discrimination or recognition of facial expression; or teaching specific skills that have repercussions for deeper *foundation elements*, such as helping a ten-year-old to finally master the production of certain phonemes that have previously been missing in his speech. As his confidence grows, he begins to join in more at school, starts to view himself as a successful communicator and is at last able to express his ideas without fear of ridicule. He begins to enjoy the communication process.

These three levels of effect are interrelated and interdependent, but each has a definite focus. Helping children to improve their speech, language and communication skills can therefore involve (and, I would argue, *should* involve) not only awareness of the interrelatedness of these levels but also a deliberate use of strategies which specifically target each one. Of course, there is also a developmental aspect to these levels, and the way in which I have distinguished the levels is not an exact science, but my suggestion is that mindful support for children of any age who have communication impairments will help to sow the seeds of future communication well-being.

Foundation elements

I have written elsewhere about the foundation elements for healthy self-esteem (see *Helping Children to Build Self-Esteem* (2nd edition) 2007, pp.24–5). I believe that we can view speech and language therapy activities as having an effect on these same seven elements, which, in turn, can be seen as further buffers against the stress of communication impairment. The seven foundation elements that I propose are listed below. The key features of these elements are based on cognitive processes, and involve *developing, knowing, recognising, believing, feeling* and *understanding*.

1. Self-knowledge

This is about finding out who 'I' am and where I fit into the social world around me. It involves:

- Understanding differences and commonalities – for example, how I am different from others in looks and character, or how I can have an interest in common with others.

- Knowing that I can sometimes behave in different ways according to the situation that I'm in and that I have many aspects to my personality.

- Developing and maintaining my personal values.

- Developing a sense of my personal history – my own 'story'.

2. Self and others

This involves:

- Understanding the joys and challenges of relationships: learning to trust and to cooperate with others; being able to see things from other people's perspective (empathy) and developing an understanding of how they might see me; learning respect and tolerance for other people's views.

- Developing and maintaining my own identity as a separate person while still recognising the natural interdependence of relationships and developing a sense of my family/cultural 'story'.

- Developing emotional intelligence – understanding my emotions and being aware of the ways in which I express them; developing a degree of emotional resilience; knowing that I can choose how to express my emotions rather than deny or repress them or act in an inappropriate way; recognising other people's emotions; distinguishing my feelings from those of others.

3. Self-acceptance

This involves:

- Knowing my own strengths, recognising what can't be changed and recognising areas that I find difficult and may want to work on. This includes accepting that it is natural to make mistakes and that this is sometimes how we learn best.

- Feeling OK about my physical body.

4. Self-reliance

This involves:

- Knowing how to take care of myself, both physically and emotionally.

- Building a measure of independence and self-motivation; believing that I have mastery over my life and can meet challenges as and when they arise.

- Reducing my reliance on other people's opinions and evaluations.

5. Self-expression

This involves:

- Understanding that my interactions reflect my beliefs about myself and about others.

- Developing creativity in self-expression and recognising and celebrating the unique and diverse ways in which we each express who we are.

6. Self-confidence

This involves:

- Knowing that my opinions, thoughts and actions have value and that I have the right to express them.

- Developing my knowledge and abilities so that I feel able to experiment with different methods of problem solving and can be flexible enough to alter my strategies if needed.

- Feeling strong enough to accept challenges and make choices.

- Feeling secure enough in myself to be able to cope with the unexpected.

7. Self-awareness

Self-awareness is the cornerstone of realistic self-evaluation. It involves:

- Developing the ability to be focused in the here and now rather than absorbed in negative thoughts about the past or future.

- Understanding my emotions so that I am aware of my feelings as they arise.

- Understanding that emotional, mental and physical changes are a natural part of my life and that I have choices about how I change and develop.

Core communication abilities

The *core communication abilities* within this framework centre on concepts of 'control', 'adaptability' and 'effectiveness'. They include:

- Self-control – a child's ability to have some control over his feelings and thoughts and the ways in which he expresses them; the ability to tolerate waiting and manage impulsivity.

- Effective listening – the ability to really hear what others are saying and to reflect on what is heard. This includes attention control.

- Effective observation – the ability to observe and reflect on non-verbal aspects of interactions.

- Imagination – the ability to imagine is an important aspect of creativity and also of empathy: the ability to see things from another person's point of view and to be aware of others' needs.

- Mutuality – the ability to understand the sharing that is involved in communication; the ability to cooperate and negotiate effectively.

- Perseverance – the ability to keep going with difficult communication tasks and to overcome obstacles.

- Adaptability – the ability to adapt to new situations and changes in communication contexts; being able to monitor and adjust actions, feelings and thoughts according to realistic assessments of personal progress.

Specific speech, language and communication skills

By *specific skills* I am referring to the behaviours which, in effect, *demonstrate* the core communication abilities. For example, in relation to being able to cooperate and negotiate successfully in a verbal exchange, any or all of the following specific skills may be utilised:

- initiating and ending an interaction

- asking/answering questions

- making requests

- taking turns in conversation

- giving personal information

- explaining/giving instructions

- using strategies for following complex instructions

- encouraging and reinforcing others

- keeping an interaction going/staying on the subject

- acknowledging the actions of others and giving/receiving feedback

- being appropriate and timely in interactions

- showing awareness of appropriate personal space (proximity to others).

Working within this framework of foundation elements, core communication abilities and specific speech, language and communication skills encourages us to be mindful of the therapeutic effects at all levels. If we are clear about what we are doing and why we are doing it, we are also much more likely to come up with innovative and creative ideas that will help children to develop communication well-being.

The structure of the activities

The basic activities in Part Two have been selected from several sources. Most of them have been used by me or by colleagues in the teaching and therapy professions; a few are ideas adapted from art therapy, teamwork and party activity books. Further ideas can also be found in *Helping Children to Build Self-Esteem* (Plummer 2007a) and *Social Skills Games for Children* (Plummer 2008b).

Each activity is followed by ideas for adaptations to get you started. Once again, I would like to place emphasis on the fact that these ideas and adaptations are presented only as a spur to encourage you to be imaginatively creative in a way that suits your personal therapeutic or teaching style and the developmental levels and learning styles of the children with whom you work.

The suggestions for foundation elements (E), abilities (A) and specific skills (S) which might be targeted during each activity have been limited to just one of each, but the potential usage is, of course, much greater. There is therefore space for you to add other possibilities relevant to your own focus of work. By familiarising yourself with the framework outlined above, the interplay of the levels will soon become apparent. Undoubtedly, the more often you use each activity, the more you will want to add to each list.

Suggestions for further discussion are also included for older and more able children, although it is important to remember that the activity itself is the main vehicle of learning, and therefore I suggest that you do not give more time to a discussion than you do to the activity itself.

In contrast to some of the games books I have written (*Social Skills Games for Children*, *Anger Management Games for Children* and *Self-Esteem Games for Children*), I have not included recommendations for age ranges, timings and optimal group sizes here. This is because the emphasis of this book is on encouraging practitioners and parents/carers to adapt the basic activities and to be creative in the ways in which they are used in different settings and with different children.

Chapter 2

Communication Well-Being

It is in our very nature to engage with others, to communicate our thoughts, needs and feelings in whatever way we are able. For many children, this act of communication, which so many of us take for granted, becomes a lifelong struggle. Without the right support, children with speech, language and communication difficulties and needs may also lose or fail to discover the joy that comes with communicating effectively. Speaking to others becomes something to fear, to avoid at all costs or, at the very least, is a stressful and unpleasant experience.

The consequences of the stress of living with communication impairment for both the child and her family should not be underestimated. In recent years there has been a great deal of research into child and adolescent stress, coping and resilience which indicates that stress effects are rarely the result of single acute life events. It appears that the main risks arise from 'events that are part of chronic or recurrent adversities' (Rutter 1996, p.376). Persistent communication difficulties will surely come under this category. We should remember, however, that we are not passive recipients of stressful events. We constantly interact with our environment and will invariably attempt to control, modify or avoid persistent stressors, or, where this is not possible, we will do our best to cope with the adverse effects of stress.

Risk, resilience and developmental stages

Risk

When we think about the possible anxieties that children with SLCN might be facing, the risk of these children developing some degree of emotional and/or behavioural difficulties becomes clear, and my own clinical experience confirmed this over and over again. The stress risks are multiple. Even relatively mild impairment can have far-reaching effects on self-esteem, interpersonal relationships and classroom performance.

The child with a speech or language difficulty will undoubtedly have countless experiences of not understanding what is being said to her and/or others not understanding what she is saying. She may have people look at her blankly, ask

'What did she say?' over her head or perhaps laugh at her speech efforts or tease her. The child who stutters, for example, is often acutely aware of the effect that her struggle to speak may be having on some of her listeners – effects ranging from impatience to mirth, sympathy and sometimes physical tension. Each of these experiences has potential to erode her self-esteem, and since levels of self-esteem play an extensive part in determining the way we behave, learn and relate to other people, she is likely to find friendships and other social relationships effortful. Indeed, there have been several studies showing that children with specific language impairment (SLI) often experience concurrent difficulties with social and behavioural development (e.g. Botting and Conti-Ramsden 2000; Conti-Ramsden and Botting 2004). Mistakes in interpreting and using different aspects of communication can lead to feelings of isolation and confusion and this can have long-term consequences for emotional well-being.

We know that children with delayed or disordered speech and language development often have literacy and numeracy problems (e.g. Snowling, Bishop and Stothard 2000). They are also particularly vulnerable to being victims of crime, being bullied or bullying others, and they are at risk of developing antisocial behaviour which can lead to truancy and exclusion from school. Some will go on to develop mental health difficulties in later life.

Sadly, although children with communication difficulties may well have average or above-average intelligence, others (adults as well as peers) often view them as 'not very bright'. Once this concept has been conveyed to the child she may become resigned to it and begin to underachieve because this fits in with how she is expected to behave.

Not only do children take note of other people's comments, they also need to develop the ability to use language in a way that helps them to define their successes and limitations. For those who have limited speech or language skills, 'the inability to negotiate with others verbally, to stake one's claim to attributes that others are ignoring, or to deny an attribution that seems unfair, for example, means that the elaboration of self-concepts is impeded' (Dalton 1994, p.3).

Research conducted with a group of young offenders (Bryan 2004) confirmed that high levels of speech, language and communication difficulties are found among the young offender population. For example, 23 per cent of the sample studied by Bryan scored significantly below the acceptable limits for their age on language comprehension. Davies *et al.* (2004) suggest that 35 per cent of young offenders probably have speaking and listening skills below level 1 of the National Curriculum.

There has been some research (Jerome *et al.* 2002) which suggests that young children (up to about nine years of age) with SLI do not tend to evaluate themselves as negatively as we might predict, but that by the age of 10 children with SLI appear to be more likely to view themselves negatively in 'scholastic competence, social acceptance, and behavioural conduct' than their peers with typical language development. However, in contrast, it has been well documented that even very young children can demonstrate low self-esteem if their life experience has emphasised negative attributes (e.g. Harter 1999).

There are many possible reasons why the younger age group may not always be reporting negative evaluations. Harter points out that, at a young age, self-evaluations tend to involve polar opposites of good and bad. This could mean that some instruments used to assess self-esteem may not be sensitive enough to pick up true perceptions; young children may be 'in denial', not yet ready emotionally or cognitively to realise the depth of difficulties they are facing; there may be confusion between the ideal and real self, or reluctance to reveal their true perceptions to investigators; they may be comparing themselves to other children in similar situations; or they may indeed have reached a point of 'healthy adaptation' (Harter 1999, p.139). Other influences include the possibility that peers may be more accepting at this younger age and therefore less likely to make negative comments. Similarly, parental support, praise and encouragement that emphasises strengths may be having a stronger effect in the early years.

Resilience

Despite the many risks, however, some children show remarkable resilience. There is much written about risk and resilience in relation to physical and mental well-being. To me, resilience in the context of speech and language difficulties is also about developing and maintaining *communication well-being* – in other words, a sense of enjoyment and effectiveness in the act of communication despite any specific impairment that may be present.

Levels of resilience partly depend on a child's ability to moderate stress and on her coping strategies. These in turn will be influenced by personal temperament, environment, social support and past experiences. When we are under stress, we will naturally attempt to self-regulate (e.g. Leventhal, Brisette and Leventhal 2003). We engage in a variety of coping strategies which may be behavioural (e.g. avoiding a situation, taking physical exercise), emotional (e.g. talking it over with a good friend) or cognitive (e.g. rethinking how I view the stressor). Some of these strategies are adaptive – they work for us; others are maladaptive – they take us off in the wrong direction.

In his exploration of individual variability in resilience and susceptibility to stress, Garmezy notes that adaptive and maladaptive behaviours are in fact 'inextricably linked…the two are not dichotomous but truly overlapping' (Garmezy 1996, pp.13–14). The type of adaptation utilised by an individual appears to be reliant on personal and situational contexts and is influenced by certain personal 'protective' factors which are highlighted by Garmezy as including: '(1) stable care; (2) problem-solving abilities; (3) attractiveness to peers and adults; (4) manifest competence and perceived efficacy; (5) identification with competent role models; (6) planfulness and aspiration' (Masten, Best and Garmezy 1990, cited in Garmezy 1996, p.14). These personal factors interact with other stress-buffering factors such as environmental resources (e.g. supportive social relationships) so that the efficacy of one may be dependent on or relate to the degree to which another is present (Gore and Eckenrode 1996).

Helping children to improve their communication skills and communication well-being can effectively be placed in the context of Garmezy's six protective factors:

1. Stable care

The existence of a strong and stable or 'secure' attachment (Ainsworth, Bell and Stayton 1971; Ainsworth *et al.* 1978) between a child and her carer during the early years has been linked to the development of language skills (e.g. Allen and Wasserman 1985) and is known to be of prime importance in the establishment of an effective emotion regulation system and resistance to the harmful effects of stress (e.g. Cooper, Shaver and Collins 1998).

Early attachment experiences affect the development of the prefrontal cortex – the area of the brain that deals with feelings and with social interactions. The prefrontal cortex plays a vital role in inhibiting or regulating the more primitive responses of the amygdala – the area of the brain that deals with the fear and self-defence systems – and is most vulnerable to outside influences during its critical period of development in the first four years of life.

Without a well-developed prefrontal cortex, children will not only have difficulty with self-control and self-regulation but also with the ability to feel 'connected' to others. It has been found that some four-year-olds who have been brought up in chaotic and stressful environments (e.g. where there has been severe neglect or abuse) have a measurably smaller prefrontal cortex compared to four-year-olds who have experienced a nurturing environment. These children show clear signs of lack of social competence, an inability to manage stress and the inability to see things from another child's viewpoint (Gerhardt 2004).

Children who have SLI and associated attachment difficulties will have different ways of coping with stress and of responding to adult support in a therapy situation. For example, some children may not be able to tolerate adult intervention in their play. Others may constantly seek adult reassurance that what they are doing is OK. Practitioners need to be aware of the type of coping strategy used by each child and be able to work within the child's comfort zone in order to minimise her stress before attempting to increase or withdraw the amount of support that the child finds comfortable. Games and play activities provide children with the freedom and security of joining in to the degree that they feel able and gradually extending their participation and self-direction.

2. Problem-solving abilities

In order to cope with communication stress successfully, children will need to engage in some degree of problem solving, and yet because of the very nature of language disorder/delay, this is a difficult task for many children. Focusing on problem-solving strategies and the 'language' of problem solving is therefore an important aspect of communication therapy. Games and activities which foster creative problem solving are an important part of therapy.

3. Attractiveness to peers and adults

If we take this to mean attractiveness in terms of building friendships, then it can be seen that some children with SLCN will have considerable difficulties in an integrated environment. Language is our means of formulating and conveying our self-concept to others. Children with SLCN often have difficulty in elaborating their self-concept (Dalton 1994). As they grow older, and particularly during adolescence, they have a greater tendency to view themselves as less attractive to their peers in terms of social competence, and, as already mentioned, peers and adults have a tendency to view children with SLCN as generally less able than their peers who do not have any communication impairment. Helping children to 'shine' in collaborative, non-competitive activities with their peers is therefore another important component of therapy.

4. Manifest competence and perceived efficacy

Communication well-being involves actual competency or mastery of skills and also positive perception of self-efficacy: the *belief* that we are capable of doing something and that we can influence events that affect our lives (Bandura 1977, 1989). Bandura suggested that people who have perceptions of high self-efficacy often do better than those who have equal ability but less belief in themselves. They are more likely to persevere with difficult tasks, use more effective problem-solving strategies, set themselves more demanding goals and focus less on the possible consequences of failure. Playing non-competitive games and creative activities can be an excellent way of encouraging a sense of self-efficacy. In terms of actual competency, it is important to establish with children what competency truly means in terms of different skills. It can be all too easy to foster unrealistic expectations in children so that they cannot tolerate natural mistakes.

At the same time, we also need to continue to foster enjoyment of the communication process. The sheer pleasure of making strange noises or listening to 'beautiful' words or 'funny' words, even if you do not have the mastery to say them, is an important aspect of communication well-being – we need to encourage children to celebrate the wonder of words. (for example keep a dictionary for words that they love and put favourite words in an 'awe and wonder' box!)

5. Identification with competent role models

There are many instances of children and adults with speech and language difficulties coping with remarkable fortitude. The arrival of blogs and video diaries has helped enormously in highlighting these tales of courage and adaptability, and I would encourage use of appropriate sources to help motivate youngsters wherever possible. Also, when children are engaged together in whole-group activities and simply having 'fun' together while learning, those with specific difficulties can engage with more competent peers without risk of failure.

6. Planfulness and aspiration

The ability to set goals and to 'aspire' to greater achievements is, of course, a prime motivator. The children with whom we work often need support in setting realistic goals with small, manageable steps, but even unrealistic goals can be acknowledged as a heartfelt wish or an exciting thought. Again, play and non-competitive activities can encourage children to learn how to formulate steps towards a goal and to imagine situations *as if* they had really happened.

The therapist's role in supporting communication well-being

It is clear that speech and language therapists have a role to play in supporting at least some of the above factors that have been proposed as buffers to communication stress. Certainly, within the therapy context we need to be attuned to the possibilities available to us for highlighting such factors and helping children and families to strengthen appropriate coping mechanisms. We need to be aware of what it means to each individual child to live with her specific communication difficulty and what that difficulty means within the family.

Since most children with SLCN will at some point in their lives experience intense frustration and anxiety associated with communication, it is not surprising that this can also occur so easily in therapy situations. We must therefore be aware of how therapy programmes have potential to increase this anxiety unless the context in which they are delivered is carefully structured to take this into account. Some of the fears that children may be facing in even the simplest of therapy activities include worries about personal outcome (will I fail?), evaluation apprehension (will I embarrass myself?), feelings of low general efficacy (will this help?), and low self-efficacy (will I feel useless?).

Chapters 3 and 4 explore some of the ways in which we might utilise play and how we might structure the emotional environment in order to help children to feel listened to, understood and supported in their communication attempts.

Chapter 3

Play as a Therapeutic Tool for Communication

A friend recently drew my attention to the fact that the word 'school' has its roots in the ancient Greek word *schole*, meaning 'leisure' or time set aside from daily routines for learning about yourself and for gaining insights into life. Although we now see leisure as something quite different to this, the link between leisure and learning is one which is perhaps very apt in the exploration of the importance of play.

Play is a natural childhood activity, and a child's imagination is a valuable inner resource which can be used to foster creative thinking, healthy self-esteem and the ability to interact successfully with others. The universality of play and traditional games highlights the developmental importance of this aspect of children's learning. From early babyhood, through our childhood years and often into adulthood (through sports activities, for example), play is how we find out about ourselves and the world. Play of one sort or another provides invaluable opportunities for children to learn through imitation, to experience the consequences of their actions and to experiment with different skills and different outcomes without fear of failure or being judged unfavourably by others. It is also through play that children can expand and consolidate their language skills.

Psychologist Catherine Garvey suggests that:

> Because playing is voluntarily controlled activity (executed in a way in which imperfect achievement is minimally dangerous), its effects are probably intricately related to the child's mastery and integration of her experiences... When the behavior is next performed in a non play mode, it may be more skilled, better integrated, and associated with a richer or wider range of meaning. In this way play can contribute to the expertise of the player and to his effectiveness in the non play world (Garvey 1990, p.167–168)

Vivian Paley has also documented many crucial observations of the importance of children's play. As a nursery teacher, she became increasingly aware of how children in her classes placed a great deal of emphasis on things that happened during play activities – it was the themes that arose during play that they were most likely to want to discuss. In her wonderful book *The Boy Who Would Be a Helicopter*, Paley observes that children's rites and images in play:

> seem mainly concerned with the uses of friendship and fantasy to avoid fear and loneliness and to establish a comfortable relationship with people and events. In play, the child says, 'I can *do* this well; I can *be* this effectively; I *understand* what is happening to me and to other children'. (Paley 1991, p.10)

We now know that pleasurable, playful experiences also affect the chemical balance and neurological make-up of the brain. For example, imaginative and creative play is known to lower levels of stress chemicals, enabling children to deal more successfully with stressful situations (see discussion on risk and resilience in Chapter 2). Gentle rough-and-tumble play and laughter are also known to have anti-stress effects, activating the brain's emotion-regulating centres and causing the release of opioids, the natural brain chemicals that induce feelings of pleasure and well-being (Sunderland 2006).

Play during childhood can stimulate a 'playful' approach to life at a later age, including the ability to bring humour and fun to relationships and to see life's difficulties as challenges rather than insurmountable obstacles. It helps children to develop social awareness and conscience and creates opportunities to explore concepts of fairness and equality.

I like David Cohen's exclamation: 'Ponder the irony! Children are the experts at play, play is their work and yet we, long-out-of-practice oldies, think we can teach them how to play!' (Cohen 1993, p.13) and Vivian Paley's expansion on this: 'We were taught to say that play is the work of children. But watching and listening to them, I saw that play was nothing less than Truth and Life' (Paley 1991, p.17).

Competition and cooperation

I am sure that each of us has had experience of being involved in games and activities that just didn't seem to work, even though they had been carefully chosen to suit the needs of particular children. Picture the following imaginary scenario:

> Seven-year-old Adam is joining in with a group game of 'By the sea' – an active, fun game chosen by group facilitator Maggie to help the children to let off steam. The group has previously been concentrating on a written task which proved quite difficult for Adam. 'You're already OUT, Adam!' comes the indignant cry from Ben. 'You can't keep joining in when you're ALREADY

OUT!' Maggie invites Adam to stand near her and help her to decide who is out next time. Adam reluctantly agrees but during the next round insists that Ben is 'out'. The game quickly deteriorates into a series of denials and second chances. Finally an exhausted Maggie brings things to an early close when she spots Adam systematically emptying out the contents of the sand tray in the far corner of the room. (From *Self-Esteem Games for Children*, Plummer 2007b)

Why is it that some games seem to work well with one group and not with another? I believe that one of the main reasons lies in how well the person who is facilitating the games understands the importance of the game process and how powerful this process can be. Of course, games played as energisers or treats can be exciting and fun and a source of immense pleasure for the players. Occasionally, however, they can also be sheer torture for the quiet child, the child who has difficulty in understanding the rules of games, the child who is already full of pent-up frustration or anxiety, or who fears being 'left out' or losing yet again. In these circumstances some games may heighten feelings of low self-esteem in children and trigger uncomfortably intense or inappropriate emotional responses.

In contrast, a well-chosen game played with awareness on the part of the facilitator can be an incredibly effective instrument for supporting a child's emergent sense of self and for helping him to tolerate frustration and learn to cooperate with his peers.

Games provide a fun way of learning serious ideas and important life skills. When they are facilitated by adults, they should always be played mindfully and with integrity. We need to be fully aware of why we are playing the games that we have chosen, fully conscious of the possible effects that playing such games might have, and fully 'present' with the children in order to understand their ways of responding and interacting and to appreciate the spontaneous learning that is occurring within and between participants.

The games and activities in this book are all non-competitive; the enjoyment and the challenge come from the process itself rather than from winning. Although competitive activities can form an important part of a child's learning once he is ready to engage in them and does so by his own choice, the ability to cope successfully in competition with peers is a tricky hurdle to negotiate and one which will complicate the process of focusing on the building of other skills. Younger children and those who are particularly vulnerable to low self-esteem often find win-or-lose games extremely difficult to manage. For such children, the anticipation of the 'rewards' of winning might be so great that the disappointment of losing has an equally dramatic effect on their mood. In order to enjoy and benefit from competitive games, they will therefore need first to develop a degree of emotional resilience, competence and self-efficacy, all of which can be fostered initially through non-competitive activities. Competition against oneself can, of course, be very rewarding. Trying to beat your own best score is a common feature of many childhood games.

Playing games with rules

The ability to play games with rules usually emerges at around five or six years of age, although the early signs of this can be seen with very young infants (a game of peek-a-boo, for example, involves structured turn-taking to some extent, and children of three often understand the 'unspoken' rules of familiar games). By around five years of age, children are more able to tolerate waiting their turn. They are beginning to exercise self-control and are developing the ability to follow rules and conventions. They are also more able to sustain interactions with others for longer periods of time.

Games generally have clear start and finishing points and follow sequences which are accepted by the players and which can therefore be replicated at other times and in different situations. These 'process' rules provide a sense of predictability and security even when the game itself might be a bit scary, and in this way various real life issues which might be too difficult or painful to confront head-on can be played out in safety. Such games engender laughter and enjoyment whilst dealing with important life issues.

In their daily lives, children have to negotiate their way through a welter of adult-imposed rules, structures and boundaries. Sometimes these are explicit but often they are unclear or unspoken, taken for granted by the adults but a potential minefield for children who forget, don't know or don't understand them. Constant insistence on adherence to adult-imposed rules in games may similarly have a negative effect on the process, resulting in children disengaging with the games, rebelling or becoming passive. Rules should therefore be flexible enough to accommodate different types or levels of response.

A major way in which children will learn to understand and respect rules is by having experience of devising them for themselves, preferably by negotiating with others, and then trying them out. In this way they learn that games are usually only successful when everyone adheres to the rules but that there can also be differing versions and perspectives. They learn that they have choices and that others will listen to their ideas.

Older children should also be given plenty of opportunities to invent new versions of familiar games and to alter the rules of games in discussion with other group members. Experimentation with the structure of games helps children to understand the value of rules and to distinguish more easily between what works and what doesn't. Discussion with peers also provides opportunities for developing skills in negotiating and decision making. Before any alterations are made, it is, of course, important to make it clear to all players that there are certain safety and non-discriminatory rules which must always be followed.

Games sessions also need 'rules' or guidelines to help foster the feeling of trust and safety amongst those taking part and to help ensure that the group is a safe place to be. Two of the most important rules for facilitators to make clear are:

1. *Children will always be given the choice of staying in or out of the game.* For children who opt out frequently, you may want to suggest an alternative role such as timekeeper to encourage some initial involvement. For some anxious children, observing others engaging in a game without feeling in any way included could allow the build-up of negative emotions, whereas for others it gives them the opportunity to prepare themselves to join in by watching what happens and familiarising themselves with the rules.

2. *Children who are reluctant to take part straight away may choose to join in at any time by giving a signal.*

(Note: If the group appears generally restless, do not insist on continuing for a certain number of set rounds of a game; take it as an indication that it is not the right time to play this game or that it is not the right game for this group.)

Further rules should be established for the reflection/discussion time. In order for children to feel comfortable in contributing to these sessions, they need to know that their ideas and opinions are valued and that they will be listened to without judgement from others and without being interrupted. Older children should also be encouraged to explore differing opinions where appropriate, thus giving them the opportunity to debate a point constructively.

Being creative with games and activities

Bob Eberle's work in relation to creative ideas is a useful tool to use when thinking about how to adapt activities to suit children at different ages and stages and how to create new games (e.g. Eberle 2008). Based on original ideas by Alex Osborn (1953), Eberle uses SCAMPER as an acronym for strategies that can be used to make changes to existing ideas: Substitute, Combine, Adapt, Modify, Put to another use, Eliminate, Reverse. SCAMPER can be used to formulate questions we might ask ourselves in relation to therapy games and activities.

1. *Substitute.* Explore what might happen if you change something. Can the rules of the game be changed? What happens if you change one part of

the game? What if you played it in a different place and with different sized groups? What if two children were leaders together?

2. *Combine.* What happens if you combine elements? What materials could be combined? Can you combine elements of two different games to make a third option? Can you bring two unlikely groups of children together?

3. *Adjust.* How can you adjust a game/activity to suit different levels of ability/learning styles? What else is similar to this game/activity?

4. *Modify.* What can be modified, magnified or minified? Can you change the colours, shapes, number, size of the equipment being used?

5. *What can you put to other uses?* What can you use this game for, or piece of equipment for, other than its most obvious use?

6. *Eliminate.* What can you eliminate? What isn't needed for this group/child/learning situation?

7. *Reverse.* What can you reverse or rearrange? What if you changed the order of what you do? What if you look at this from the perspective of a different child or group? What if you let the child/children lead a whole session?

Participation

As mindful facilitators of the game process, we can make certain hypotheses about the ways in which children participate in therapy activities. First, the way a child acts and reacts in a game situation is likely to reflect his life experiences in some way and therefore also reflect how he behaves in other situations. So, without being overly analytical or too literal in our interpretations of children's behaviour during play, it is nevertheless important for us to be aware of general patterns. Are there children who take a long time to warm up to each activity? Are there some who are 'taking over'? What happens when children become frustrated or cannot tolerate waiting their turn? Are they able to recognise personal achievements and those of others? Do they behave independently or always look to others to take the lead? Are they able to take on different roles at different times or for different types of activity?

A second hypothesis that we might make centres on children's capacity for change. Working within a humanistic framework, we can approach the playing of games and participation in therapy activities with the assumption that all children, whatever their current abilities, have within them the resources, and therefore the potential, for change and growth. However small or large the changes might be, the ability to respond with a degree of flexibility in different situations and the ability to learn from active participation is part of what it is to be human.

We should also remember that each child's attitude to different therapy activities, his degree of participation and his enjoyment of the activity will change over time as he matures and learns.

Valuing children's views about a therapy session is also likely to foster increased motivation to engage more fully in the learning process, and their comments about a particular game/activity could guide you in choosing another one to address that specific issue/skill.

Setting the scene

Wherever appropriate, tell the child/children what you are going to do, and how and why you are doing it, and invite any questions: 'We're going to play a story game. We need to sit in a circle. I will tell you/show you how to play. The story game will help you with your talking. Do you want to ask me about the story game?'

You might set the focus with a more detailed introduction, perhaps by telling a short story or recounting a fictitious event to illustrate a particular use or misuse of a skill. You could then introduce the chosen activity as being a way of exploring that skill. On completion of the activity, 'debrief' or discuss what happened during play. As children become used to the format, they can be encouraged to choose familiar games and activities (perhaps from a small selection of possible options) which they think might be relevant for a particular skill. This process of choosing can also engender useful discussions about how skills are learned and developed.

Humour

Some of the most successful activities that I have been involved in with children have occurred when I have made a mistake and children have laughed at the absurdities that have resulted. Although my mistakes were not deliberate, I soon learnt that occasionally injecting humour into an activity can certainly help the learning process.

Using different media

The games and activities in Part Two have been divided into sections according to different types (e.g. ball and beanbag games; paper and pencil activities) rather than according to communication skills. This will give you the opportunity to offer children a variety of activities which capitalise on different strengths and build areas which they find more challenging.

Although you may be constrained by clinic or classroom space, there should always be a variety of methods whereby children can learn different skills.

Constructing a portable tool kit can be particularly useful. For example, your tool kit might contain:

- three bean bags or equivalents

- coloured ribbon wound into a ball that can be thrown, rolled or unwound in group activities

- a soft cloth that can be used as a story shawl or a mini parachute

- inflatable dice

- an unusual musical instrument

- a silk scarf

- coloured paper and pastels

- a talking stick or unusual object for turn taking and circle games

- lollipop sticks and pipe cleaners for making puppets.

Make use of school sand play areas and water trays, incorporate outdoor activities wherever possible and let children get messy. Whatever appeals to their sense of fun and promotes their enjoyment of play (within safety limits!) should be utilised.

Chapter 4

Structuring the Emotional Environment

As already stated in Chapter 1, this book is intended as something more than a collection of activities and games. Emphasis is given to the *way* in which such activities and games are undertaken. If we engage with children in an emotionally intelligent way, then we help children to build self-efficacy and emotional resilience: we encourage communication well-being. For this reason it is important to treat every session as a new and unique experience and to make it child-centred rather than content-centred. The *value* of our expertise in therapy comes through applying that expertise in an emotionally intelligent way.

Emotional intelligence in therapy

Emotional intelligence includes the capacity for self-awareness and the ability to recognise our own feelings and those of others. It also involves the ability to motivate ourselves and to manage emotions well in ourselves and in our relationships (Goleman 1996, pp.43–4).

In the context of therapy, emotional intelligence involves two aspects: recognising our own feelings and those of the children, families and other professionals with whom we are working; and promoting an appropriate emotional state in the children in order to facilitate learning.

Interacting with emotional intelligence therefore involves structuring the emotional environment with just as much care as we structure the physical environment for learning. We can do this through taking account of motivational aspects; being explicit about roles, rules and boundaries; promoting a child-centred approach; praising in a mindful and appropriate way; using solution-focused language; and ensuring that we are using reflection to good effect.

Motivation to learn: being ready, willing and able

A healthy communication eco-system (the social environment and the various communication relationships with which each child engages) both fosters and depends on readiness, willingness and ability. The 'ready, willing and able' maxim has been adopted for use in motivational interviewing (e.g. Miller and Rollnick 2002) and is one which I feel is very relevant for children who are struggling to communicate effectively and for the families who are supporting them.

Miller and Rollnick, the proponents of motivational interviewing, highlight these three aspects as being primary components of motivation for change. We might ask ourselves: is the child (and are parents/carers) *ready* for this change – is it top of their priority list right now? Is the child developmentally ready? To what extent is the child/carer *willing* to change – how much do they desire the change? And how confident are the child and carer that they are *able* to change?

If we are ready, willing and able, then this in turn leads to increased engagement with the process of change. If a child and her carers are not engaged with the therapy process, then we might predict that learning and generalisation will be minimised. With this in mind, it is important that the strategies that we use are aimed at supporting, engaging and motivating children and their families/carers.

Roles and boundaries

For some children who are new to therapy or who are joining a therapy group, taking part in activities can be scary and we need to spend time building trust amongst group members and between ourselves and the children we are supporting. Trust is most easily established if roles, rules and boundaries are clearly outlined both as part of individual therapy and at the start of a group. This can help children to feel 'contained' and safe. An example of a clear time boundary might be: 'Today the games session will be ten minutes long and when we have finished the game we will do X.' Or: 'Every morning we will play one game during circle time and then we will…'

It is also the facilitator's task to demonstrate a firm but fair approach in order to prevent difficulties arising – for example, some children being consistently very dominant or ridiculed by others because they do not understand the game rules. It is crucial that all group members (including family groups) understand the importance of supporting each other's participation – even games that purport to be non-competitive can sometimes be played in a competitive, even aggressive way unless there are clear guidelines. Again, this will enable the children to feel safe within the structure of the activities and allow them the opportunity to experiment and explore, to expand their self-concept and to self-evaluate without fear of being judged harshly.

Individual differences in social customs, beliefs and behaviours should also be acknowledged and an atmosphere of open discussion should be encouraged. Children need to feel safe enough to be able to say what is the 'norm' for their family or culture when this differs from the general consensus of the group.

Because of the multilayered nature of therapy, there will be multiple roles for therapists/facilitators. Although these may change and evolve over time, deciding on your role and the purpose of the activities you choose will help you to structure and reflect on the sessions more effectively. Possible roles might include several of the following at any one time:

- role model
- teacher/provider of challenges
- facilitator/encourager/enabler
- supporter/helper
- mediator/arbitrator
- observer
- participant
- researcher/information gatherer/assessor
- supervisor
- provider of fun
- ideas person
- timekeeper.

Consider whether or not the roles you are taking on conflict in any way and, if so, which one you need to concentrate on. Perhaps a second person is needed to take a different perspective or role? For example, can you be facilitator/encourager and also record information about how individuals are coping with different aspects of a particular activity?

In which role are you happiest? Do you feel most comfortable as 'provider of fun' or in the 'teaching' role?

What about the roles of the children? These too may change and evolve over time so that group members each have the opportunity to be the facilitator or the 'ideas' person or 'teacher'. Those who feel unable to join in with a particular game may enjoy being timekeeper or observer. Children who understand the rules of games and can explain these to others may naturally take on the role of arbitrator or facilitator, leading others in making choices and in ensuring that the rules are understood and followed by all participants. This is a valuable skill which can be encouraged during many of the activities suggested in this book.

Monitoring of rules by the participants themselves is an important aspect of play. Children who would normally find this role difficult can be gradually encouraged and supported in leading and monitoring fairly. Those children who have plenty of experience in arbitrating and leading games can also be encouraged to support this process by stepping back to allow others to have a go.

Child-centred therapy

Carl Rogers, the originator of 'person-centred' therapy, believed that each of us has a natural tendency to strive to achieve our full potential in life and he proposed that there are certain conditions which will promote this tendency. These became known as the 'core conditions' for a successful therapeutic alliance, but Rogers also made it clear that he felt such conditions were valid for *all* human relationships. He believed that if he maintained a relationship characterised on his part by congruence ('a genuineness and transparency, in which I am my real feelings'), unconditional positive regard ('warm acceptance of and prizing of the other person as a separate individual') and empathy ('a sensitive ability to see his world and himself as he sees them'), then the other person in the relationship would be more self-directing and self-confident and able to cope with life's problems 'more comfortably' (Rogers 1961, pp.37–8).

Most of us recognise the importance of these core conditions in terms of our own relationships, but in our busy lives, and often because of our own early life experiences, we can easily forget some of the ways in which we can actually demonstrate these principles to children.

Over the years I have found that there are also two very practical strategies which can help children to recognise their own worth and to be more self-directed. The first involves a clear demonstration that we understand, value and respect their feelings. The second involves giving genuine, realistic and specific praise which reflects our belief in each child's unique capabilities.

Valuing feelings

In structured therapy activities, children who have difficulty in understanding and expressing their feelings verbally can begin to explore difficult emotions in safety and with the spirit of 'play'. In this way, games help children to recognise that others often have similar experiences and emotions. However, we should also be aware that when children are in groups together, they will all have feelings about the feelings of the other children! Displays of anxiety, anger or upset by one child may trigger feelings of anxiety, anger or distress in another. It will be the facilitator's task to help children to regulate their emotions within the group and demonstrate a calm way of reacting to any displays of strong emotion.

How do we help children to be constructively aware of their emotions? The key is to acknowledge and validate feelings. For example, if a child with a hearing difficulty says 'I hate this game, it's stupid', think about the feeling behind the comment. Avoid interpretations but comment on what you see, hear and feel. Aim to support rather than rescue. Responses such as 'But everyone else is enjoying it, I'm sure you will too', 'You haven't tried it yet, let's have a go together' or 'That's OK, you can sit this one out if you like' would probably all get a negative reaction. Such comments, though well-meaning, do not help the child to understand her own feelings more fully or to discover her own solutions in situations that she finds difficult (see p.44 for further exploration of solution-focused talk).

Making a hypothesis about the feeling behind the words and offering an appropriate comment ('It's a very noisy game and I noticed that it's hard to hear the instructions sometimes. I wonder if it would be more fun for you to stand nearer the teacher') can help the child to feel understood and is more likely to lead to her making adjustments in her self-evaluation.

Praise

Praise and demonstration of pleasure in a child's abilities, perseverance, sense of fun and so on can be an excellent motivator for continued change and development, but children are usually very good at spotting praise that is not genuine and will be quick to reject it if it doesn't fit with how they see themselves. Also, unrealistic or unjustified praise could set a child up for experiencing low self-esteem if she tries to do things before she is ready, or if it leads to her developing unrealistically high expectations of what she can achieve. Even when we do offer genuine praise, adults have an unfortunate tendency to add a qualification of some sort! Such qualified praise might go something like:

'That's a lovely picture – but you've forgotten his eyes!'

'What a great way to share – if only you'd done that this morning, you wouldn't have got into a fight!'

'Well done for helping out – why can't you always do that without getting grumpy?'

'I noticed that you were being really helpful when Sam was upset – you'd usually get cross with him, wouldn't you?'

Similarly, it can be all too easy to offer praise that indicates the lesser achievements of others. An award for the fastest worker or best listener, for example, suggests that there are others who are not so good at this and also gives little scope for further development ('If I am already the best, I don't need to think about that any more!').

So here are some alternatives:

- The most effective approach is to use genuine specific, descriptive praise whenever possible: 'I liked the way you really listened to what Josh had to say about following the rules of the game' or 'I noticed you were being very helpful when Sam got upset and that really worked because he calmed down straight away!' or 'Your "problem" picture really shows me what it must feel like to be worried about your talking. This is what I call thoughtful' or 'You were ace at noticing your worry thoughts and keeping them controlled today'.

- Acknowledge difficulties and empathise with the feelings: 'It looked as if it was hard for you to wait your turn. You had lots of great ideas to share! That must have been really frustrating for you!'

- Encourage children to give descriptive praise to others: 'What did you like about the way that Josh told us that?'

- Encourage descriptive *self*-praise: 'I asked a really good question in class today' or 'I talked to someone new at break time and it was hard but I felt good afterwards'.

- Expressing your admiration can also enable a child to self-evaluate in a wonderfully productive way: 'That's fantastic! How did you know how to do that?' or 'I had no idea that you knew about the planets/were so artistic/could make a kite. Was that hard to learn?' or 'Tim said that you always remember people's birthdays – that's really impressive! How do you manage to do that?'

- Give non-verbal signals of approval and encouragement. A 'thumbs up', a wink or a smile across a room can be helpful for children who are anxious. You can show that you understand how they feel without rushing in to rescue them.

- Christine Durham, in her book *Chasing Ideas* (Durham 2006), describes a useful way to make praise a fun interaction for older children. She suggests the use of acronyms and abbreviations such as VIP (very important proposition) or IT (insightful thinking). This could start as a game in itself

– perhaps taking familiar acronyms and familiar sayings and encouraging children to make up 'secret' messages about their communication skills. For example, VIP could be 'Very Imaginative Problem-solver' or ACE could be 'A Cool Example'. Giving a child a 'thumbs up' sign and saying 'ACE' then becomes even more meaningful and fun!

- Encourage children to reflect on what happens during certain chosen activities and during daily routines, picking up on the encounters and strategies that are working well and, in particular, any moments of difficulty that have been successfully negotiated.

- Use memory aids if necessary to help you to remember ideas that children have come up with during some of the activities in this book. Comment on these at a later time to show that you have really thought about what was said.

- A clear demonstration that we value children as unique individuals can be conveyed in the simplest of ways. Telling a child that we enjoy her company, or love talking with her emphasises the fact that she has a positive 'effect' on us simply by being who she is and not because of what she does or doesn't say or do.

- Remember the often quoted (but worth repeating!) warning to avoid 'labelling' – even if this is just a private thought. For example, instead of thinking of a child as 'shy', try to be more specific: 'At the moment she is unsure of herself when she first arrives somewhere new. It takes her a while to build the confidence to talk to new people. It might help if we practised some things that she could say.'

- Although some children might find it difficult to recognise their current abilities, achievements and talents, this is always a good starting point before moving on to thinking about targets for learning and future goals for self-development. It is important to continue to acknowledge and celebrate current strengths. Children generally have very little time in their lives to celebrate where they are at before moving on to the next challenge, the next learning target, the next physical achievement – almost as though we are telling them 'Yes, well done, but that's still not quite good enough'!

There is one more aspect of praise which is significant in terms of group processes (this includes families). The *absence* of praise may have almost as much of a detrimental effect on some vulnerable children as the giving of negative comments. When a vulnerable child hears others in the group being praised by an important adult for attributes and talents which she admires but does not feel she possesses (and is not being praised for), this gives indirect information to that child about how the adult views her. So although we need to keep praise realistic and honest, we also need to find out what really matters to individual children. What do they most admire in others? What would they most like to be praised for? How could we support them in nurturing their wishes in this respect?

Using solution-focused language

When children are having difficulty in changing behaviour and thought patterns, engaging them in solution-focused strategies can be extremely useful. Solution-focused brief therapy (SFBT) is a recognised therapeutic and teaching approach (see www.sfbta.org for further information). As its name suggests, this approach encourages solution-based rather than problem-based dialogue. Some of the basic assumptions and styles of interaction inherent in SFBT are easily incorporated into daily contacts with children and can make a big difference to how a child begins to see herself and the possibility of change.

In essence, solution-focused communication arises quite naturally from a philosophy that emphasizes the skills, strengths and resources of individuals. If we believe that a child is capable of change, that she has the resources for change and she doesn't always need to be told what to do, then our communications will reflect this.

Solution-focused language also reflects the assumption that the child will already be doing something that will help her towards her goal, however small that step might be. Let's take the example used earlier of a child with a hearing impairment not wanting to join in with games. If this child is evidently frustrated and angry, an individual discussion after the games session might go something like this:

Child: I hate these games.

Adult: Sometimes you really hate the games we're playing.

Child: Yeah. No one ever listens to me (*kicks the table leg forcefully*).

(The use of words such as 'never', 'always' and 'no one' adds justification to the anger: 'If no one ever takes any notice of me, then I am justified in feeling angry'.)

Adult: Some people don't listen to you and then you get angry.

(Anger is acknowledged and deliberately linked with a particular trigger in order to suggest an alternative to the sense of constant anger.)

Child: Yeah!

Adult: So when we're playing these games and you're *not* angry, how does that feel?

(This introduces the idea of the exception to the rule.)

Child: Dunno. OK, I guess.

Adult: You feel OK sometimes. I wonder what will be different when you are feeling OK in the games more often?

(This assumes that the change will happen and helps the child to begin to 'flesh out' the details of what that will be like and what she will do in order to make it happen. The more details 'the preferred future' can be given, the more likely it is to happen.)

In this shortened version of a possible interaction, the adult has acknowledged the problem but has introduced the possibility for change by using words such as 'sometimes' and by looking for the exception to the feeling of constant anger. It is important for the child to focus on what she *will* be feeling, doing and thinking, not on what she doesn't want. Other questions might therefore include:

What else will you notice?

How will your teacher/classmates know that you are feeling OK?

What will happen then?

Reflective practice

Reflective practice is a firmly established element of speech and language therapy provision and should be an automatic consideration for the activities in this book. The following questions are some that I have found helpful when planning and reviewing sessions:

- What is my role as the facilitator?
- How will I set the tone of the session/introduce the activities in a fun way?
- Why are we playing these particular games? What are my aims/intended outcomes?
- How will I know if I've achieved my aims/outcomes?
- What are my personal feelings about these activities? If I was this child's age, would I enjoy playing these games?

- Are the activities appropriate for the age/cultural background of the child/children in the group?

- Do I know the 'rules' of the games?

- Who (if anyone) in the group will find the activities difficult/challenging/easy?

- Do I need to adapt the activities in any way to allow/encourage full participation of all group members?

- What back-up strategies will I need?

- How will I handle behaviour that is potentially disruptive to the group?

- Am I aware of why this behaviour might occur?

- If the group is large or diverse in needs, do I have a 'support' person available?

- What will I do if a child knows a different version of a game and wants to play that? (You might suggest, for example, that you play the child's version next time or it might be appropriate to share different versions at the time and abandon one of the other games you had planned.)

- Is this the right time for the game(s)/activities?

- Is the room the right temperature?

- Am I feeling up to it?

After completion of a therapy session it is useful to take a few moments as soon as you can to reflect on the activities. What went well? Was there anything that was difficult to monitor? What skills did you use? What did you enjoy about the activities? What did the children most enjoy? Was each activity of an appropriate length? Was the level right for the child/the whole group? Did you introduce and summarise activities effectively? Did you achieve your objectives? If you were to do a similar session again, would you change it in any way? Why? What would you do differently? How would you extend/alter each activity to move the child/group on to the next stage when they are ready? Were there any issues raised concerning age, cultural or gender differences that will need to be addressed?

Remember, reflective practice is not about being judgemental about your own abilities. It is about reflecting on your skills and on your learning and on your ways of navigating any difficulties.

Chapter 5
Working in Different Settings

Bhavik, aged four, has a marked delay in his language development. He is struggling at school and has frequent tantrums born of frustration. It is becoming increasingly difficult for the teaching staff to engage Bhavik in any whole-class activities.

Jamie, aged seven, has just moved up to the juniors. He is having difficulty with learning to read. He appears bright but is falling behind in all areas of the curriculum.

Helen, aged 12, has just moved to a new school. She has stammered since she was three years old, but her stammer has become interiorised. She avoids certain situations and people and is constantly changing her words in order to hide her stammering. The anxiety of having to meet new people and explain about her speech is resulting in bouts of sickness and severe headaches.

The activities and games in this book are suitable for children from five to twelve years of age. However, with appropriate adaptations, many of them can also be used successfully with older children. In the school setting they will fit into a wide selection of personal, social and health education (PSHE) and other learning objectives. They can be used to teach and enhance a variety of skills at primary level and to reinforce strategies for successful communication and social interaction during the vulnerable period of transition to secondary education. The material can be incorporated into individual behaviour plans (IBPs) and can be used to target specific aspects of individual education plans (IEPs).

The activities can also be used to compliment other approaches to speech and language development and support.

Crucially, all the ideas can be used at home by families. The central role played by parents and carers (and often by the wider family network) in supporting a child's communication development is, of course, tremendously important. The special time shared during a fun therapy game can be a boost to helping family members to understand each other, understand their child's communication needs, show their love and strengthen their relationship. Sharing moments of laughter, problem solving and creativity during games can be rewarding and reaffirming for everyone concerned.

The ways in which the activities are adapted and incorporated into family life and into educational and therapy approaches can and should vary according to the setting and according to the needs, strengths and experiences of the children. Each adult who facilitates these activities will naturally bring his or her own personality, imagination, expertise and knowledge to the sessions and create something new from the basic format.

Projects and themes

Don't be afraid to follow child-initiated ideas. In fact, if children are able to engage in a discussion about outcomes and interests, then I recommend that they be involved in planning sessions with you. This might take the form of asking a child at the end of one session whether or not they would like to continue the same theme for the next session or choose a different one. Children as young as four who do not have a specific language impairment are perfectly capable of putting forward ideas about planning class sessions and themes, so do bear this in mind, especially when working collaboratively in schools.

For example, a foundation year teacher told me recently that she had asked her class of 30 children what they would most like to learn about during the coming week. They chose dinosaurs – a fabulous theme, full of rich words to positively savour! They then talked about how they could research this, and everyone went away to find books in the library or information on the internet. During the week they made dinosaur landscapes, learnt about how dinosaurs digested their food, looked at relative size and weight, became archaeologists in the sandpit, created new dinosaurs at the 'awe and wonder' table and learnt a hundred other things while 'playing'.

At the end of each day they reviewed what they had learnt by doing a round of 'I didn't know that…'. This teacher reported that the excitement about what they were learning was tangible; children couldn't wait to start the day and everyone moved on in terms of individual targets, including a child with SLI.

This clearly demonstrates the concept of collaborative working: teachers, parents, children and therapists all working together in order to:

- foster an atmosphere where children can be actively engaged in the learning process

- encourage spontaneity and creativity

- help focus thought processes

- develop higher-level thinking skills

- provide an opportunity to develop and practise organisational and self-monitoring skills

- encourage tolerance and respect of other people's ideas

- provide a vehicle for positive interaction with peers

- enhance awareness of cause and effect.

Learning in this way is fun and engages the children in a positive and productive way. Giving an instruction to a child such as 'put the pencil under the table' in order to help them to learn prepositions is meaningless unless it is in the context of something interesting happening. Hiding a dinosaur bone under a rock for the archaeologist to find is much more fun!

Individual or group therapy?

The choice of whether to work with a child on a one-to-one basis or in a group of two or more will, of course, largely depend on the results of your assessment and on the type of provision being offered. Perhaps you will be working in a community clinic setting or in schools/children's centres, etc.

We also need to be aware of developmental ages and stages. Again, in relation to stress, Pless and Stein suggest that:

> ...it is entirely possible that strategies that appear highly effective in one age group will be found to be ineffective in another... Although the notion that developmental stage may be an essential mediator of intervention effects is a compelling consideration, its salience is likely to vary greatly depending on the nature of the intervention. ...For example, peer counselling is probably only feasible among teenagers, whereas parent support groups should have few, if any, age boundaries. (Pless and Stein 1994, p.343)

One aspect to be particularly aware of is how we cope with groups and monitor group processes. Larger groups will undoubtedly benefit from having at least two facilitators. It is very difficult to 'hold' a group and to be aware of everything that is going on within and between all the group members if you are working on your own. Having two facilitators gives you the chance to share ideas, keep better track of what is happening and obviously share the responsibility for planning, carrying out and evaluating the sessions.

It is also important for each facilitator to be able to reflect on his or her skills as a group leader and to be able to debrief at the end of each session. This is much harder if you are only able to do this infrequently with a peer or at a scheduled supervision session.

Taking time to reflect on the group process and on the session can enable facilitators to deal with the challenges and joys of a group more effectively and to monitor facilitation skills in ways that are most likely to support the children. An added bonus, of course, is that constructive discussions with a co-facilitator help to strengthen personal feelings of competency and self-worth.

Advantages of working with a group

Groups offer the opportunity for:

- on-the-spot peer support which could be extended beyond the life of the group

- pooling resources and ideas

- learning and building on social skills

- reducing the facilitator's 'teacher'/'magician' status

- encouraging independence

- active experimentation to try out new ways of 'being'

- active engagement in the learning process

- spontaneity and creativity as participants try out ideas with more than one person – generalisation of learning

- encouraging tolerance and respect of other people's ideas

- experience of positive interaction with peers

- taking the focus away from individuals (but needing to be more aware of children not taking full part)

- activities to be incorporated into whole-class activities.

The disadvantages are mainly in respect of the time and energy needed by group facilitators!:

- Groups take a lot of organising in the early stages. You will need a variety of activities and materials to allow for a variety of learning styles.

- You need to be aware of how groups function and that you will be encouraging 'group-esteem' as well as individual self-esteem.

- It may take some members a long time to 'find their feet' in a group.

- It may be more tempting to give advice or take over the group during group discussions than if you were working with someone one to one.

Some general principles to consider

- Feeling part of a group and being accepted and appreciated by a group gives us a sense of belonging and helps us to feel good about ourselves, especially when our internal reserves are low. Sometimes, however, we may find ourselves behaving in ways that don't truly reflect our self-concept in order to *appear* to fit in with a group. Children can be particularly vulnerable to this sort of peer pressure. They may try to 'fit in' with a group because they think they ought to or because it's 'cool' or it's exciting. There may be times when this is OK and also times when it's not OK – when trying to fit in leads to them feeling awkward or unhappy. It is important to acknowledge this natural wish to feel accepted and liked and to explore successful ways of achieving this. Talk about different areas of 'commonality' – for example, any other groups that the children might be members of, such as school groups, family groups, sports teams, etc. The aim is to help the children to look beyond physical things that they might have in common to such things as leisure interests and common aims.

- Because new groups need time to get to know each other, it is useful to build up a repertoire of group 'gelling' games and warm-up games. Devoting some specific time to these games will help children to feel more relaxed about sharing their ideas and taking part in cooperative activities. See, for example, *Social Skills Games for Children* (Plummer 2008b).

- Aim to promote communication between group members. Children should be encouraged to direct their questions and comments to each other with the facilitator keeping things moving.

- Introduce only a limited amount of new material each session. Encourage personal contributions from older children about their own experiences of using the strategies that have been discussed and tried out in the sessions.

- Look for opportunities to allow more reticent children to speak.

- Be sensitive but firm with children who tend to dominate the group.

- It is also useful to establish a set of group 'rules', and to remind the group of these periodically if needed.

- Make sure that there is opportunity for a celebration in the last session. This could so easily be missed out because of lack of time or because it is not given due importance. It is, however, very important to complete the group in this way. It defines the end of the life of the group as it stands. It gives weight to acknowledging everyone's achievements and it shows that enjoyment and celebration are part of the learning process.

And whether you are working with a group or an individual:

- Use a variety of activities to target particular foundation elements, core abilities and specific skills; use each activity to work on several aspects. The repetition of games and activities will aid the process of generalization to real life situations.

- Be clear about your criteria for success – don't be tempted to alter the goal posts during an activity. You can always reflect on necessary changes afterwards.

- Capitalise on each child's areas of strength when devising new activities and adapting old ones.

- Make learning functional, fun and rewarding.

Part Two

Activities and Games

Chapter 6

Beyond the Beanbag!

General tips

- Use a variety of large, soft objects which can be caught and thrown easily, especially by children who have some difficulty with coordinating their movements. For example: a soft ball with a silk scarf attached (if a child misses 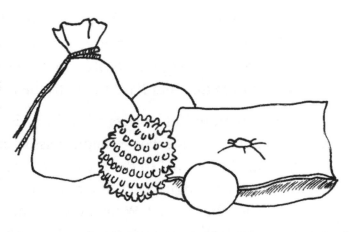 the ball she might still be able to catch the scarf), a soft rubber 'spiky' ball, a soft cushion, a cotton or silk bag filled with polystyrene balls or cotton wool.

- Some children may find it easier to sit in a circle or a pair and roll a ball from one to the other rather than try to catch a fast-moving object such as a bean bag.

- Use extra-large balls, such as those used for fitness training, to roll across the floor to each other. Think about the size carefully in relation to the object of the game. In a circle, using a very large ball may prevent children from looking at each other, or indeed actually seeing everyone over the top of the ball. This would not promote a feeling of connectedness in the group!

- Make your own beanbags out of socks (or involve children in making their own) – just fill them with dried beans and tie a knot in the top, or fill a bag with enough sand to make it 'squidgy' but not too heavy (this also makes a good 'stress ball'). Make sure these home-made versions are tied securely, and obviously be aware of safety issues.

- Demonstrate how to throw gently! Allow children the chance to throw the soft ball or bag with force at a wall or across a wide space but not directly at other children. Compare this to throwing gently. Talk about the difference.

- Use a different selection of bags and balls at different times – for example, a bag made of felt or fake fur, or a felt ball with a bell inside or filled with lavender. Give children the chance to explore the weight, texture, smell and colour of the soft balls and bags before they play the games.

- Use bags made of fabric that represents green slime or a hot yellow sun – the 'hot' or 'slimy' bag is more likely to be passed quickly from one player to the next!

- If children are finding it too difficult to throw or catch a beanbag, allow them to pass the bag more gently or to stand nearer the target. These games are not a test of dexterity and it is more important that children learn about turn taking and have fun with the activities.

- Use beautiful objects which will in themselves engender rich language. For example, pass around a shell. First say a quality related to the shell. Then use the shell for expanding on language in a variety of ways. Where might the shell be found? What lived in the shell? What shape is the shell (texture/size/weight). Use the shell as a type of 'talking stick'. When the shell comes to you, say one thing you like about being you (remember that children have the option of passing on these turn-taking games).

- Throw a large ball of wool, ribbon or string, or use silk scarves which have been tied together and rolled into a ball. Each child holds on to part of this and throws or passes the ball on to the next person, forming a 'web' of connections. This can help to promote a sense of being connected with other members of the group. It can also work well with just two people, passing the ball back and forth to make a stronger and stronger connection.

- If you are running a regular group with the same children, write all their names on the balls, bags or ribbons that you use so that they have a sense of group cohesion.

- For games such as *3D noughts and crosses* (see game 1), make a permanent grid on a large sheet of plastic that can be used repeatedly for working on different concepts.

1. 3D noughts and crosses

Foundation elements, abilities and skills

- ☑ self and others (E)   ☑
- ☑ self-control (A)   ☑
- ☑ taking turns (S)   ☑

The basic activity

Draw out a large chalk grid of nine squares (3x3) on the playground or mark it out on the floor using masking tape. Mark three bags with a cross and three with a circle. Take turns to toss the beanbags onto the grid, trying to get three crosses or three circles in a row.

Adaptations

- Place coloured squares or pictures of everyday objects, animal pictures, sound pictures, etc. in the grid. When a child manages to get a beanbag into a square, she names the colour/object/make the sound.

- If a player's beanbag lands where another beanbag is, then the first bag is removed.

- Make up a sentence or a longer story using the first set of three objects that are connected.

- If you are working with a group of six or more children, then each child can hold her beanbag with the nought/cross clearly visible and jump into the squares instead of throwing the bag (can be played as a team game or simply for fun with no attempt at having a winning team).

- Sequence the sounds/blend them together.

- Throw three beanbags randomly onto the grid, and wherever they land fully in a square, say the sounds/name the objects or make up a story.

Expansion ideas

- How easy or difficult is it to get three noughts or three crosses in a row? Why is this?

- Is it easier to work as a team or on your own? Why?

2. Beginnings and endings (1)

See also *Beginnings and endings (2)*, p.76.

Foundation elements, abilities and skills

- ☑ self-confidence (E)   ☑
- ☑ effective listening (A)   ☑
- ☑ beginning and ending an interaction (S)   ☑

The basic activity

Players sit in a circle and throw a bean bag or soft ball to each other. The catcher thinks of a phrase or question that could be used to start off an interaction such as 'Did you stay for football practice last night?', 'Can I play too?' or 'I'm not sure how to do this. Can you help me please?' When everyone has had a turn, players think of ways to end an interaction such as 'Bye. See you tomorrow' or 'Thanks for your help'.

Adaptations

- If a player is unable to think of something, then they can choose from two suggestions offered by the facilitator or by another player.
- Work in pairs to devise a complete conversation of four sentences.
- Instead of a beanbag or ball, pass a mobile phone. The facilitator says 'I have a direct line to… (space control, the producer of EastEnders, a master wizard, a famous footballer, etc). What do you want to ask him/her?' and hands over the mobile phone.
- Use a microphone for 'audience participation' in a question-and-answer session.

Expansion ideas

- Do conversations always start with a question?
- Do conversations end with questions?
- What happens if no one asks a question during a conversation?

3. Pass a gift

See also *Praise indeed*, p.79.

Foundation elements, abilities and skills

- ☑ self-acceptance (E)　　　　　☑
- ☑ imagination/empathy (A)　　　☑
- ☑ giving and receiving praise (S)　☑

The basic activity

Use a large glitter ball or a beautiful/unusual object. Pass the ball to each other (or around the group). Whoever is holding it praises someone else and passes them the ball. This is best done in sequence around the circle to start with until you feel that children can praise each other in random order and not leave anyone out.

Adaptations

- Brainstorm praises before you start.
- Let children take turns in choosing the object to be used.
- Choose different methods of praising on different occasions or for different levels of ability (see notes on praising in Part One, pp.41–44).
- Encourage children to say 'thank you' when praised or to give a non-verbal acknowledgement of the praise.

Expansion ideas

- What do you feel when you give and receive praise?
- How many different ways can we praise each other?
- What would you most like to be praised for? What do you think your mother/brother/best friend would most like to be praised for?
- Is there anything you *don't* like to be praised for?

4. Skittle alley

Foundation elements, abilities and skills

☑ self-expression (E)   ☑

☑ effective listening (A)   ☑

☑ following instructions (S) ☑

The basic activity

Tape pictures, letters or words onto plastic skittles or plastic water bottles filled with a small amount of sand to make them stable. Children knock them down with a beanbag or ball when they hear the facilitator say the sound/word.

Adaptations

- This very simple activity can easily be adapted to suit differing abilities. Most obviously, you can increase/decrease the number of skittles and move them further apart or closer together.

- Use a selection of sizes of water bottle and fill them with different coloured balls/strips of paper (just enough to make them stand firmly but not too much to make them hard to knock down!). These can be used for following increasingly complex instructions such as 'Knock down the small blue skittle (bottle)' or 'IF you knock down the red skittle first, THEN you will have a free turn'. Involve the children in collecting the bottles and making the skittles.

- Fill the bottles with different weighted material and explore opposites such as 'heavy/light', 'easy/difficult', 'wet/dry', 'full/empty', 'quiet/noisy'.

- Use different coloured skittles for different parts of a sentence (e.g. blue for nouns and red for verbs). Tape words or pictures to the underneath of the skittles. The child knocks over one from each category and makes up a sentence using the revealed words.

Expansion ideas

- Use the process of making the skittles to encourage discussion around concepts of quantity, weight, stability, variation, etc.

- Talk about making words into sentences.

5. Beanbag sports

Foundation elements, abilities and skills

- ☑ self-awareness (E) ☑
- ☑ self-control (A) ☑
- ☑ auditory discrimination (S) ☑

The basic activity

- The child holds the bean bag between her feet and jumps towards a finishing line when the facilitator says a certain sound or word. She must only jump when she hears the target sound/word and must stay still when other sounds/words are used. The line can be moved nearer or further away to increase or decrease the level of difficulty.

Adaptations

- Invite children to choose their own words to listen out for. Encourage them to 'enjoy' words ('Who likes that word?', 'What is your favourite word today?').
- The child says the sound/word/sentence as they jump.
- Play this as a relay game with each child repeating the sound/word or saying a different part of a sentence.
- Have different categories of words at various changeover points along the race track (e.g. different colour bean bags for different parts of a sentence).
- When the child gets to the finish line, she says the full sentence or waits until she hears a certain sound before throwing/dropping the beanbag into a large container.

Expansion ideas

- Talk about how sounds make words and words make sentences.
- How easy/difficult is it to think about speech and do something else at the same time?

6. Uses for a beanbag

Foundation elements, abilities and skills

- ☑ self-reliance (E)   ☑
- ☑ adaptability (A)   ☑
- ☑ problem solving (S)   ☑

The basic activity

- Work in groups or pairs to brainstorm all the different things that a beanbag could be used for. Accept all ideas. Encourage children to be as inventive as possible. Prompt with specific questions if needed.

Adaptations

- Act out different uses for others to guess.
- Have a selection of different weights and sizes of beanbag. Discuss different uses for different bags.
- Limit the uses to a specific situation (e.g. uses for a beanbag on a desert island/ at a children's party/in a science lesson).

Expansion ideas

- Is it easier for you to think of ideas in a group or on your own? Why is this?
- Is it easier for you to take your time to think about things slowly or to think quickly? Why is this?
- Why is it helpful to think about unusual uses for different objects?
- Did you have the chance to say all your ideas? Did other people have some of the same ideas as you?

7. Living pelmanism

Foundation elements, abilities and skills

- ☑ self-acceptance (E)   ☑
- ☑ effective observation (A)   ☑
- ☑ using memory strategies (S)   ☑

The basic activity

(This is best played in a fairly small group to start with.)

A child is chosen to be Player 1. The rest of the children are paired up or randomly assigned words that rhyme or words that go together (e.g. bucket and spade). They will have to be able to remember their word. They then arrange themselves randomly in a circle around the first player. Player 1 throws a beanbag to two others to see if they match. The catcher says her word. If there is a match, then those two children sit down. Player 1 continues until she has found all the matches.

Adaptations

- Before Player 1 throws the beanbag, ask all the children to say their word three times.

- Players have their picture or written word clearly displayed in front of them for varying lengths of time so that Player 1 can memorise them before they are turned over and the game starts.

- The children have their pictures/words positioned so that they are not clearly visible to the thrower but can be seen as a reminder for themselves.

- Players cut out/collect their own pictures within a suggested category to use for the game.

Expansion ideas

- What helps you to remember things during a lesson at school?

- What can you do to help you to remember all the things you need to do at the weekend?

- How do you help yourself to remember your friends' birthdays?

- What would you do if you forgot your packed lunch/sports kit?

8. Closing circles

Foundation elements, abilities and skills

- ☑ self-knowledge (E)   ☑
- ☑ mutuality (A)   ☑
- ☑ sentence construction (S)   ☑

The basic activity

At the end of each session encourage children to say one brief thing about the session before they leave. Offer an idea for each child to complete in their own words. For example: 'I feel…, today I found out that…, today I felt…, my name is and I am…, I have noticed that…, I feel really good about…, my next step is…, I want to say that…, today this group has given me…'

Adaptations

- Use emotion pictures as prompts. Children choose the picture that best matches how they feel about the session.

- Offer possibilities based on your observations. For example, 'Today I think you felt very proud of how well you did. Am I right?' or 'I noticed that today it was difficult for you to concentrate when we played *x* but you really enjoyed the game of *y*'.

Expansion ideas

- Do you set yourself goals to work towards? What would you most like to achieve by the end of next week? Next month? Next term? How will you know when you've achieved it? How will other people know that you've achieved it?

Some more ideas

- Player 1 holds on to a ball of wide ribbon which is long enough to suit the size of the group. The end of the ribbon is passed around the group so that a complete circle is made. There is a knot in the ribbon. Any child can choose to speak when the knot reaches them.

- Player 1 starts off a story, then throws a ball of ribbon to someone else in the circle, keeping hold of one end. The catcher continues the story and holds on to the next piece of ribbon, throwing the main ball to someone else and so on until the story is completed or the ribbon runs out.

- Throw and catch an imaginary object. Try and guess the qualities of the object as it is passed from one child to another. Is it big and heavy? Small and light? Spiky? Sticky? Smelly?

- Pass around an imaginary hat. When anyone puts on this hat, they can become a famous person or a character from a well-known story. They must then try to show who they are through mime. The rest of the group tries to guess who the wearer is pretending to be.

Chapter 7

Big Space Activities and Games

General tips

- Outdoor activities can add a great deal to the process of learning speech, language and communication skills and can be incorporated into the outdoor learning curriculum for younger children. As with all games and activities that involve the use of equipment or a high level of physical action (running, etc.), these activities need careful supervision.

- Many of the following games can also be played indoors, in a large hall, for example, where children won't bump into furniture or fall on a slippery floor.

- Where 'tagging' is involved, ensure that children do this gently.

- Go BIG – use giant inflatable dice, giant snakes and ladders mats, etc. There are lots of outdoor commercial games available that can be adapted for speech and language games.

- Wherever possible, also use some materials from the immediate environment as part of the activity.

- Always end outdoor activities with a quiet time to help the children to calm down and absorb what they have learnt.

1. Duck duck goose

Foundation elements, abilities and skills

- ☑ self and others (E)   ☑
- ☑ self-control (A)   ☑
- ☑ auditory discrimination (S)   ☑

The basic activity

This well-known party game can be adapted for numerous different therapy goals. Children sit or stand in a circle facing each other. One child is the fox. He walks slowly around the outside of the circle, tapping each child on the shoulder and saying 'duck'. When the fox taps a child and says 'goose', the fox and the goose run around the circle in opposite directions to see who can get back to the empty place first. The player left out of the circle then walks slowly around the outside and chooses another person. Play continues until every child has had the chance to be a goose and a fox or until the children have had enough!

Adaptations

- The fox walks around the circle using different adjectives to describe the ducks (e.g. 'big duck', 'little duck', 'happy duck', 'sad duck') and the children listen out for a pre-chosen adjective to start running (e.g. 'quick duck').

- The adult or child walks around the circle saying words from a particular category (e.g. animals). When they name something from another category (e.g. fruit) the race begins.

- Children listen for the 'odd one out' (e.g. k, k, k, g).

- If 'duck' or 'goose' are difficult words and you are not specifically working on t/d, k/g, try having a cow that chases the sheep instead and use animal sounds (moo and baa!).

- If you are working with just one child, take turns to walk slowly around each other saying a word/sound/phrase, then instead of touching someone, when there is a change both of you run to a marked point some distance away. The first one there becomes the fox.

- Use characters from a story. The children listen out for their own name or for the name of one of the characters.

- Players hop in opposite directions to get to the available space.

- Mark the empty space with a picture so that the fox and the goose don't get confused about where they are headed.

Expansion ideas

- How easy or difficult was it for you to wait to be picked? Do you normally wait until someone says something to you before joining in with a conversation or a discussion in class? How is this similar/different to waiting your turn in a game?

- How can you help others to join a group that you are already in?

- What do you do when you want to join a group of people who are already playing or working together? What could you say to the group?

- When is it easy to join a group? When might it be difficult?

2. Splodge tag

Foundation elements, abilities and skills

☑ self and others (E) ☑

☑ mutuality/cooperation (A) ☑

☑ effective observation (S) ☑

The basic activity

The game starts in the same way as a normal tag game. The first player to be the 'tagger' runs after the rest of the group. When he manages to tag another player, they join hands. These two players then try to tag a third and then a fourth player who also join up with them. As soon as there is a group of four players together, they split into two sets and each set goes off to tag two more players and so on until there is only one person left who has not yet been tagged. If the game is to continue, this player starts off as the new tagger.

Adaptations

- Player 1 starts off a splodge by tagging children who are wearing the same colour T-shirt or who have something else in common, such as short hair. When all children in this group are tagged, the facilitator calls out the next category and so on until all the players are part of one big 'splodge'.

Expansion ideas

- This game only works well if players cooperate fully with each other. Was it difficult or easy for small groups to cooperate?

- Did the last person to be tagged in the big splodge have anything in common with the first person to be tagged? What other things did the splodge members have in common apart from physical features?

- How did you decide in which direction to run? Were you all trying to run at the same pace?

- What were the small splodges trying to do? Was it important to stay together or to catch someone else?

3. Zoo too

Foundation elements, abilities and skills

☑ self-reliance (E)   ☑

☑ perseverance (A)   ☑

☑ vocabulary knowledge (S)   ☑

The basic activity

Mark out two lines a few yards apart from each other. One child is the zookeeper. He walks around between the two lines, making sure that all the other children (the animals) remain behind the lines. All the other children are different animals in the zoo but the zookeeper doesn't know their identity. The animals pace around behind the lines. The zookeeper calls out the names of animals – as many as he can think of. As soon as he calls the name of one of the animals behind the lines, that child tries to run to the other side before being caught by the zookeeper. If he is caught he must 'freeze'. Play continues until all children are 'frozen'.

Adaptations

- Swap zookeepers after a certain number of animals have been caught.
- Give the children animal cards at the start of the game to help them to remember which animal they are.
- Have more than one of each animal.
- This game can be adapted for a variety of concepts and given a different theme – for example, a space crew could catch floating letters!

Expansion ideas

- What does the zookeeper have to be particularly good at? What does he need to know?
- How did the zookeeper work out which animals were in the zoo?
- What do the 'animals' need to be good at? How can these skills help us when we are talking to each other?

4. Outdoor fruit salad

Foundation elements, abilities and skills

☑ self-knowledge (E)   ☑

☑ effective listening (A)   ☑

☑ using memory strategies (S)   ☑

The basic activity

This is a fast-paced game that can easily be adapted to suit different likes and dislikes. For that reason, it can be played many times in different formats and is always a favourite amongst groups of active children!

Stand in a large circle with one person standing in the centre. Each person chooses the name of a different fruit. The person in the centre calls out two fruits. These two children swap places and the caller tries to reach one of the empty spaces before the other person gets there. If the caller says 'fruit salad', everyone swaps places! The person left standing is the next caller.

Adaptations

- Swap places if you have something in common (e.g. had cereal for breakfast this morning, have brown eyes). Everyone swaps when the caller says something that he knows everyone has in common.

- Play Motorway, using car names or Zookeeper, using animal names. And anything else that comes in groups!

- For larger groups and the younger age range, have a limited number of items so that there is more than one child for each one (four apples, four bananas, etc.). This can get quite hectic with lots of children running across the circle at the same time, so take care!

Expansion ideas

- Do different children like different versions? Why?
- Why can some games be frustrating for some players?
- What do all games have in common?
- Debate the pros and cons of competitive and non-competitive/cooperative games.

5. What can I see?

Foundation elements, abilities and skills

☑ self-confidence (E)   ☑

☑ effective observation (A)   ☑

☑ understanding and using prepositions (S)   ☑

The basic activity

Mark out a square in the woods, playground, garden or indoors. One child stands in the middle and looks all the way round, naming whatever he can see without moving from the spot. He then closes his eyes and remembers what was behind him, in front of him, under his feet, above his head, etc. in response to questions from the adult/other players.

Adaptations

- Hang objects in the lower branches of a tree so that the children really have to look to find them. Once they have found them all, they then close their eyes and try to recall them.

- Try to remember items on a shopping list by imagining them hanging on a tree.

Expansion ideas

- What skills are needed for this game? How might these skills be helpful when we talk with each other?
- What is the difference between looking, seeing and observing?
- What strategies do you use to help you to remember things?

6. Calling cards

Foundation elements, abilities and skills

☑ self-expression (E)   ☑

☑ perseverance (A)   ☑

☑ understanding opposites (S)   ☑

The basic activity

Players select one card each from a pile of cards showing common objects that go together, such as a card showing a toothbrush and a card showing toothpaste, or a letter and a postbox. Players stand in a circle and everyone calls out what is on their card at the same time. The aim is for all the players to find their 'partner'.

Adaptations

- Players find their opposite (e.g. up/down, big/little, hot/cold).
- Players find two others in the same category (e.g. happy, excited, elated).
- Half the group has cards with questions on such as 'Why is the girl laughing?' The other half of the group has 'because' cards – 'because her friend has told her a funny joke'.

Expansion ideas

- What is the difference between hearing and listening?
- How do you know when someone has listened to what you have said?
- How do you *show* that you are listening?
- What sort of things do people *say* to indicate that they are listening?
- Is it easier or harder for you to listen/talk in a large group? Why is that?

7. Shepherds and sheep

Foundation elements, abilities and skills

- ☑ self-expression (E)   ☑
- ☑ imagination (A)   ☑
- ☑ monitoring volume and pitch (S)   ☑

The basic activity

Children work together in pairs. One is the shepherd and the other is the sheep. The sheep wears a blindfold or covers his eyes. The shepherd steers the sheep into its pen (a square marked out with masking tape) by using changes in pitch or volume only – for example, humming with a rising pitch for 'go left', a falling pitch for 'go right' and a level pitch for 'straight ahead'. Once the sheep is safely in the pen, the pairs swap over but start from a different position in the room, playground, etc.

Adaptations

- Use more subtle, appropriate pitch changes for 'yes', 'nearly right', 'wrong way', etc.
- Steer the sheep to their pen using changes in volume, different vowel sounds or clapping.
- If children do not like wearing a tight blindfold, try using a large paper carrier bag instead.

Expansion ideas

- How many different ways can you say the word 'no'? How does changing the pitch of your speech alter the meaning of the word?
- What is sarcasm? How can you tell when someone is being sarcastic?

8. Blindfold obstacle course

Foundation elements, abilities and skills

- ☑ self-reliance (E)   ☑
- ☑ imagination (A)   ☑
- ☑ giving instructions (S)   ☑

The basic activity

One player is blindfolded and must navigate his way over an obstacle course, relying on instructions given by the other players.

Adaptations

- Work in pairs, with the 'seeing' partner walking next to the player who is blindfolded.

- Players form a large 'centipede' by holding on to each other around the waist or placing their hands on the shoulders of the person in front of them. The centipede walks around a large obstacle course (this could be a series of 'ponds' or 'centipede traps' made of pieces of paper). Everyone keeps their eyes shut except the person at the front who has to lead them safely through and give instructions as they go, keeping careful track of what is happening to all parts of the centipede.

Expansion ideas

- Is it easy or difficult to give instructions to someone who is blindfolded? Why?

- Is it easier to give instructions to one person or to a group? Why?

- Did you feel more comfortable giving instructions or following instructions? Why was that?

- What speech goals are you working towards at the moment? Are there any obstacles in your way? How might you overcome some of these obstacles?

Some more ideas

- Spread a roll of plain wallpaper across the playground. Invite children to draw whatever they want (or specify a theme) and to cover as much of the paper as possible. Encourage discussion during and after the activity.

- Play hopscotch with different sounds represented in each square.

- Construct an obstacle course using natural objects collected from outdoors. Give instructions – 'jump over the pile of pine cones', etc. Help children to give instructions to each other.

- Set up a concept-based treasure hunt.

- Play Kim's game with objects from nature which the child has collected and named beforehand.

- Make a sculpture out of natural materials and then talk about it. Spend ten minutes collecting items and give pairs of children ten minutes to make their sculpture. Then everyone looks at everyone else's work. Take photos of the sculptures to talk about later.

- See also Chapter 13, *Parachute Games*

Chapter 8

Being Creative with Paper and Pencil Activities

General tips

• The activities in this section include several written sheets. Most of them are adapted and extended versions of a selection of activity sheets from *Helping Children to Build Self-Esteem* (Plummer 2007a). However, please keep in mind that the learning emphasis of this current book is very much to do with play rather than the completion of written work. Activity sheets can be a very useful tool in many situations but they do need to be used sparingly and in a structured way. Wherever possible, encourage children to draw rather than write and to work together rather than to sit quietly completing work on their own. This sharing and talking can be a highly effective and motivating way of learning for most children. It also, of course, helps to foster effective use and understanding of social communication, providing opportunities for encouraging collaborative, respectful relationships.

• Ensure that you have choices of different coloured paper and a selection of crayons, pastels, charcoal, etc. for drawings. It is important to give children the opportunity to experiment with drawing images of different sizes and to use different media. Try using giant pencils and pens for drawing on rolls of plain wallpaper and miniature crayons for drawing on sticky notelets.

• Always ask children for permission to show their work to the group or to other adults. Don't assume that it will always be OK to do so.

1. Beginnings and endings (2)

See also *Beginnings and endings (1)*, p.58

Foundation elements, abilities and skills

- ☑ self-confidence (E)   ☑
- ☑ imagination (A)   ☑
- ☑ sequencing ideas (S)   ☑

The basic activity

Possible beginnings and endings of conversations are written on cards and placed in two piles. Pairs of players pick one from each pile. They have five minutes to prepare a conversation that makes use of the beginning and ending written on the cards. Pairs then demonstrate their conversation to the whole group.

Adaptations

- Pairs choose a card from each pile and have a spontaneous 60 second conversation using both cards.
- Use the first and last picture cards from sets of sequencing cards. Pairs tell the whole sequence, making up the parts that are missing.

Expansion ideas

- Did pairs stay on the same topic for their conversation?
- What helps you to stay on the subject?
- What happens if one person in the conversation suddenly changes the topic?

2. Cartoons

Foundation elements, abilities and skills

- ☑ self and others (E)   ☑
- ☑ mutuality/negotiation (A)   ☑
- ☑ problem solving (S)   ☑

The basic activity

Players divide into small groups. Each group collaborates to make a cartoon or a collage of a scene depicting an interaction where something has gone wrong or there is at least one person who is feeling 'left out' or anxious. Groups then share their cartoons and try to guess what each other's pictures represent.

Adaptation

- Players divide into small groups and devise a one-minute silent play, depicting a situation that needs to be resolved. They then act out their plays for the rest of the group to guess the situation.

Expansion ideas

- Talk about differing viewpoints and different interpretations of the pictures and plays.
- Was there any indication of bias or stereotyping? How are these relevant to the ability to cooperate and negotiate?

3. Conversation drawings

Foundation elements, abilities and skills

- ☑ self-acceptance (E)   ☑
- ☑ imagination (A)   ☑
- ☑ non-verbal communication (S) ☑

The basic activity

Players work in pairs to construct a conversation through making squiggles and shapes with paint or crayons on the same piece of paper. Each player uses one colour and takes turns to draw their part of the conversation. Players must keep to their own half of the paper.

Adaptations

- Players construct 'happy' conversations.
- Players construct angry conversations or 'I'm worried' conversations. Finish with a resolution and a calming-down for these two interactions.
- Players work in groups of three.

- Two pairs of players construct their own conversation at opposite ends of a large piece of paper. After one or two minutes the pairs join up to share a conversation between all four players.

- Spread a roll of plain wallpaper across a large space (the school playground is ideal for this) so that players can move around and have 'art conversations' with as many different people as possible, joining groups, starting new groups or talking to just one other person at a time.

Expansion ideas

- What skills do you have that help you to join conversations and to start new conversations?

- What happens if people talk at the same time as each other?

- What happens if lots of people want to join the same conversation?

4. Emotion sensations

Foundation elements, abilities and skills

☑ self and others (E)   ☑

☑ imagination/creative thinking (A)   ☑

☑ giving instructions (S)   ☑

This requires some preparation by the facilitator beforehand.

The basic activity

Divide the group into two halves. Groups A and B then work in different rooms or in different parts of the same room but must not look at what the other group is doing. Within each group, players work in pairs or threes to draw round each other's body outline on large pieces of paper. Players use pictures from comics, catalogues, magazines, etc. to 'clothe' their own body outline with shapes and colours or objects to represent how their body feels when they experience a particular emotion, such as nervousness, happiness, anger or frustration.

Group A tries to guess who each of the pictures belongs to in group B and vice versa.

Adaptations

- Once clothed, add words, headlines and catchphrases to represent useful and not useful aspects of anger.

- Make a joint picture for one emotion, each player adding a different physical symptom.

Expansion ideas

- When you look at all the figures, can you see anything that some of them have in common? What are the main differences?

- When might a feeling of nervousness be useful?

- What feelings might cause similar sensations in your body (e.g. a knotted stomach could be excitement or anxiety, clenched fists could be a linked with anger or determination)?

- How does your body feel different when you are happy? What about when you are confident?

- If you are anxious and you change the way your body feels (e.g. by smiling and relaxing your muscles), do you start to feel a different emotion?

5. Praise indeed

See also *Pass a gift*, p.59.

Foundation elements, abilities and skills

☑ self and others (E)   ☑

☑ adaptability (A)   ☑

☑ giving and receiving praise (S)   ☑

The basic activity

Players each have a piece of paper and write their name at the bottom. The papers are collected and passed around the group for everyone to write something positive about the person named on the paper. The paper is folded over after each comment has been added so that no one sees what anyone else has written. The paper is then returned to the original player to read silently.

Adaptations

- Players have a piece of paper pinned to their back for others to write praises on.

- Players draw symbols to represent different types of praise that have already been discussed (e.g. smiley faces for 'you are a great friend' or a 'thumbs up' sign for 'you are joining in really well').

Expansion ideas

- What does it feel like to give and receive praise?

- How many different ways can we praise each other?

- What would you most like to be praised for? What do you think your mother/brother/best friend would most like to be praised for? Is there anything you *don't* like to be praised for?

6. Instructors

Foundation elements, abilities and skills

☑ self-confidence (E) ☑

☑ perseverance (A) ☑

☑ asking for clarification (S) ☑

The basic activity

Working in pairs, players take turns to explain to their partner how to draw an object such as a car, a tree or a house. The person who is drawing must follow the instructions as accurately as possible even if the end result doesn't look like the intended object. Players swap roles after a set time period.

Adaptation

- Pairs sit opposite each other with a visual barrier between them (e.g. a piece of card or an open book) so that they cannot see each other's drawings. The facilitator provides simple line drawings for instructors to describe to their partners.

Expansion ideas

- What should you do if you are uncertain about an instruction that you have been given?

- What helps you to give clear instructions?

7. Activity sheets (pp.85–101)

Foundation elements, abilities and skills

☑ self-awareness (E)   ☑

☑ imagination (A)   ☑

☑ specific skills for each activity (S)   ☑

The basic activity

Complete the written sheets together. These are divided into speaking, listening, observing, body language, conversations, taking turns and communication confidence.

Guidelines for each written sheet

7.1 ALL ABOUT HOW WE TALK (P.85)

Speech and language therapists may want to discuss this in depth, but it is useful for any group to explore how we speak in order to help children to be more tolerant of differences, and also more tolerant of their own natural mistakes.

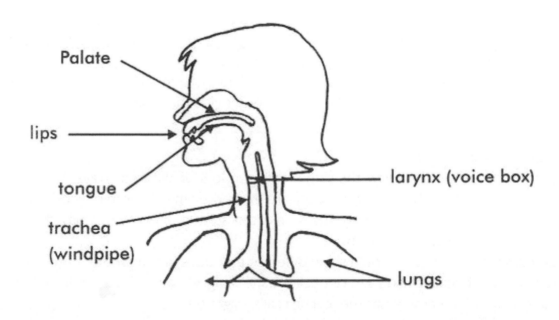

7.2 HOW DO WE SOUND WHEN WE TALK? (P.86)

This exercise helps to highlight differences and similarities in how people talk. For therapy with children who have particular speech difficulties, it could lead on to more specific discussion about what can go wrong with speech.

7.3 LISTENING SKILLS (P.88)

An activity sheet to encourage children to think about listening as a skill which requires some focusing of attention. Talk about how we can sometimes hear several things at the same time (e.g. the television, someone talking and the phone ringing), but we can choose which one to actually listen to.

7.4 LOOKING (P.89)

You will need to be aware of any cultural issues related to this. For example, it may not be appropriate for some children to use prolonged eye contact with certain adults.

7.5 KEEPING EYE CONTACT (P.90)

Ideas might include: talking for one minute on a chosen topic whilst trying to look at everyone in the group at least once; watching a video or TV programmes and observing the level of eye contact for different speakers and listeners. (See also 'Confidence groups' p.167–70.)

7.6 TAKING TURNS (P.91)

Relate your discussion to a variety of activities that require turn taking if they are to work well. For example: team games; a joint storytelling; board games; as well as conversations. Demonstrate a conversation with another adult where turn taking is not used and compare this to a conversation where you both take more or less equal turns. Encourage children to role-play this in small groups.

This activity sheet can also be used to give children with a communication difficulty the chance to say how they feel when others don't give them time to talk.

7.7 BODY TALK (P.92)

Talk about how we can show the same feeling in lots of different ways. For example, ask the children how they show that they are excited. Some children may be very active when they are excited, some may use an 'excited' gesture such as clapping their hands, and some may just smile or laugh.

Discuss the idea that we could show different emotions in almost the same way (e.g. a child could cry because she's sad or because she's angry) and we need to look for other clues to help us to know what the feeling really might be.

Act out different emotions and see if the children can guess how you are feeling. Talk about both obvious body language and more subtle things such as looking away.

7.8 CONVERSATIONS (P.94)

This activity sheet encourages children to think about wider issues other than just speech.

Talk about the wide variety of different types of conversation – with one other person, in groups, about something serious, during play, about something familiar, about something new and so on.

7.9 LET'S IMAGINE (1) (P.95)

There are several possible areas for discussion arising from this activity sheet. For example, a key social skill is knowing how to start a conversation in a natural, relaxed way. Different people will have different ways of doing this and there really are no hard and fast rules, but there are some general guidelines which can help children to get started.

7.10 LET'S IMAGINE (2) (P.96)

Use a role-play situation engineered between two adults if you think your group would pick out the important social skills, or lack of them, by watching and listening rather than from a story.

Discuss the alternative, more successful scenario, demonstrating social skills if needed.

7.11 SPEAKING IN A GROUP (P.98)

Compare and contrast groups of various sizes and who might be in each group. Do different children have different perspectives about groups?

Discuss what can be done to help the person who is talking (listen, sit still, keep good eye contact, smile, ask questions, etc.). See 'Confidence groups' p.167–170.

7.12 WHAT I FEEL ABOUT SPEAKING IN A GROUP (P.99)

Talk about what helps and what hinders. Help the children to problem-solve wherever possible.

7.13 TALKING TIMES (P.100)

It is helpful for children to understand that not only is it easier for us to talk about important things at certain times but also that it is easier for others to *listen* at certain times. This helps them to see that sometimes people may not be able to listen fully because of circumstances rather than because of dislike or rejection of the child or what she has to say.

Examples of easy and difficult times might be:

It's easy when...	It's harder when...
Mum and I are having tea together	We are rushing to get to school
I'm happy/relaxed	I'm angry/tired/upset/very excited
I'm with my best friend	Dad is watching TV
The other person is listening well	Everyone is talking at the same time
I'm in a small group	I'm in a big group
I know everyone	I don't know everyone

7.14 WHAT I LIKE ABOUT THE WAY I TALK (P.101)

This is an exercise in formulating a clear picture of successful communication skills. For example: I listened; I took turns; I asked questions.

Adaptation

Use the sheets as a basis for discussion without any writing. Encourage children to draw their ideas wherever possible.

Expansion ideas

Use the information as a basis for making links during the day to conversations in other situations.

7.1 All about how we talk

When you talk you use different parts of your mouth and throat to make speech sounds. Sounds go together to make words and words can go together to make sentences.

Everyone sounds different when they talk because we all have different-shaped mouths and throats and we move our speech muscles in slightly different ways. See if you can find out the names of some of the parts of the body that we use when we speak.

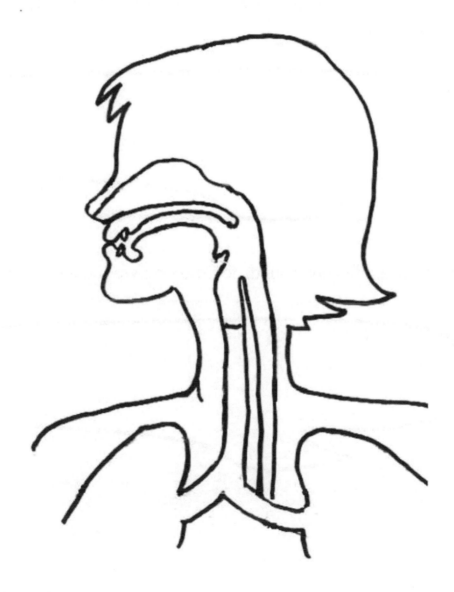

7.2 How do we sound when we talk?

People talk in lots of different ways. Some people talk very quickly. Some people talk quite slowly. Some people have a high voice and some talk with a very low, deep-sounding voice. Perhaps you've heard people talking in a different language to yours or with a different accent?

Now and then we all have difficulty getting our words out. Write the words 'my cat is black and white' in the speech bubbles and show what different speech mistakes can sound like. For example, we might mix our words up by mistake. What do you think that might sound like?

We might use different sounds for the one we meant to say:

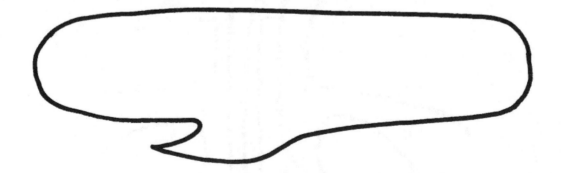

Lots of people repeat sounds or words by mistake:

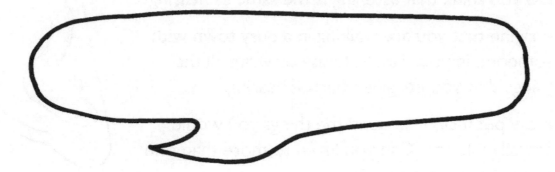

All these different ways of talking can happen to all of us a little bit and to some of us a lot.

7.3 Listening skills

Do you think that listening is the same as hearing?

Imagine that you are walking in a busy town with someone in your family. Draw or write all the things that you imagine yourself hearing.

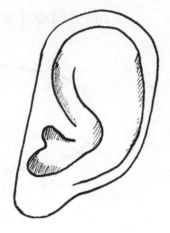

Now put a circle around the things you would actually *listen* to. Can you listen to more than one thing at the same time?

7.4 Looking

Why is it important to look at each other when we are talking?

_____

_____

Who does the most looking? Is it the person who is speaking or the person who is listening?

_____

_____

Imagine what it feels like when the person you are talking to isn't looking at you.

_____

_____

_____

_____

Imagine that you are talking to your friends and you are looking down at the floor. Imagine what your friends might be thinking.

_____

_____

_____

_____

7.5 Keeping eye contact

If people are able to look at each other easily when they are talking and listening, it is called 'keeping eye contact'.

Lots of people find this very difficult to do, especially if they are feeling a bit shy.

Keeping just the right amount of eye contact is an important part of feeling and looking confident. So now you're going to put your imagination to work by thinking up some games for practising eye contact.

Draw or write about your games here.

7.6 Taking turns

What do we mean when we talk about 'taking turns'?

_____

_____

Why is it important to take turns when we talk to each other?

_____

_____

_____

What would happen if we didn't take turns when we talked to each other? Imagine yourself having a conversation with some friends. Imagine that they are talking so much that you don't get a chance to say anything. What do you feel? What happens? What would you like to do?

_____

_____

_____

_____

_____

7.7 Body talk

Sometimes it is possible to know how someone is feeling even before they say anything.

They *show* us how they feel by the way they are standing or sitting and by the expression on their face.

What do you think the person in this picture is feeling?

_____

_____

Let's imagine

Close your eyes and imagine someone who you know. What does this person look like when they are happy?… How do they stand?… Do you think they would be moving their hands or would they be still?… What would their face be like?

Make as clear a picture as possible in your mind.

Now imagine what this person would look like if they were nervous…

What about if they were sad? …

How would they look if they were surprised?

When you are ready, see if you can draw or write about some of the things that happen when we use our bodies to talk.

7.7 Body talk – let's imagine

7.8 Conversations

What does the word 'conversation' mean?

_____

_____

_____

Draw a picture or write about a conversation you have had today. Who were you talking with? Who started the conversation? What was the conversation about? Who did the most talking? Who did the most listening? How did the conversation end?

7.9 Let's imagine (1)

Imagine that you are watching television. You are watching a programme about the two friends, Simon and Jenny. They are having a conversation about the day they went on a school trip together. What are they doing when they talk to each other? Where are they looking? How do they sound? Do they both talk at the same time?

See if you can fill the speech bubble with lots of words to describe good talking skills.

7.10 Let's imagine (2)

Mike and Bill

See if you can spot all the mistakes that Mike makes in this story.

One day Mike was mending his skateboard outside his house when Bill walked by. Mike heard Bill's footsteps and looked up. Bill waved and said, 'Hi Mike!' Mike looked back at his skateboard and carried on trying to fix the wheel.

'What are you doing?' asked Bill, kneeling down beside Mike.

'My Dad gave it to me,' said Mike. 'I think he's at work.'

'It's a great looking skateboard,' said Bill. 'How did the wheel come off?'

Mike didn't answer so Bill carried on talking.

'I used to have a skateboard but it broke when my brother tried to race it down a steep hill and it crashed into a tree at the bottom. I was really fed up and...'

'Sally isn't at home so that means we can have fish pie for tea,' Mike said suddenly.

Bill pulled a face. He wrinkled his nose and curled his lips as though he'd tasted something really disgusting. 'Oh I *love* fish pie,' he said.

'Do you?' asked Mike, not looking up.

'No, 'course not…can't stand it,' replied Bill. 'And, anyway, what's fish pie got to do with Sally?'

But Mike had fixed the wheel on his skateboard and was ready to try it out. 'Bye then,' called Bill. 'See you at school tomorrow.'

'I wonder if Bill's got that new computer game yet,' thought Mike as he raced down the path on his board.

How many mistakes did you spot?

7.11 Speaking in a group

Talking to just one person sometimes feels different from talking in a group.

Let's think about this a bit more.

Let's imagine

Imagine that you are with some friends and you are telling them about something that you did yesterday. Where do you imagine yourself being? How do you feel?

Now imagine giving a talk to your whole class. Does that feel different or the same?

Imagine that your talk has finished and it went really well. What did your classmates do that helped it to go well? What did *you* do? Write about some of the feelings.

It's hard to speak in a group when _____

_____

_____

It's easy to speak in a group when _____

_____

_____

7.12 What I feel about speaking in a group

If I were going to speak in a group, it would be OK if

_____

_____

_____

_____

_____

It would be difficult for me if _____

_____

_____

_____

_____

_____

_____

7.13 Talking times

Are there times when you feel that it's difficult for you to say what you want to say? Let's think of some times when it's easy to talk to each other and some times when it's not so easy.

It's easy to talk when...	It's harder to talk when...

7.14 What I like about the way I talk

Think about your own talking now. Think about all the things that you do when you talk, as well as how you sound.

Imagine that you have just had a long conversation with a friend. Write a list of all the things that you did to help the conversation to go well.

I imagined that I was talking to _____

This is what I did to help the conversation to go well: _____

_____

_____

_____

_____

Some more ideas

- Make a random paint blot on a large piece of paper (like ink blots). Take turns to say what it could be, then use the different ideas as the basis for a sentence/story.

- Close your eyes and create a picture. Open your eyes, add to it, talk about it. For example, a squiggle becomes a dragon.

- Play a variation of 'pin the tail on the donkey'. Make large monster shapes and stick on body parts with your eyes closed. You can then talk about different parts (e.g. 'Here's an eye on its leg!').

- Pin a plane on a map with eyes closed – talk about different countries.

- Use articles from magazines and newspapers and blank out nouns or verbs. The task is to make up a news story by replacing the missing words. Brainstorm some possible words first or replace the people in the story with animals or mythical figures.

- Make hand puppets out of plain paper bags. Make up a short play together, using the sounds/words/sentence structures that you have been practising.

- Use a set of Russian dolls with messages inside each doll stating a task for the week.

- Cut out pictures of windows and doors from magazines. Talk about what might be behind different doors or on the other side of different-shaped windows.

Chapter 9

Role Play, Storytelling and Guided Imagery

General tips

- After any of the role-play and imagery exercises, always make sure that the children have stepped out of role after completion of the activity. The release of role can be done by simple means such as asking the children to name and put away any props they have used and by getting them to shake their arms and hands and call out their own name, or count to three and turn round.

- When children are telling stories about themselves, it may be helpful to use objects/figures to give them something to hold and to focus on. A box full of lollipop sticks is an invaluable tool for this. For example, children can draw a face on a stick and talk about themselves as 'he' or 'she' or they can make an animal face and tell their story as an animal.

1. Chocolate cakes

Foundation elements, abilities and skills

☑ self-awareness (E)   ☑

☑ imagination (A)   ☑

☑ recall (S)   ☑

The basic activity

Read the imagery exercise 'Think of a chocolate cake' slowly, with plenty of pauses for the children to really explore the images. Reassure them that there is no right or wrong answer. If they seem unable to 'see' images, that's OK (in my experience, however, children are usually very quick to produce visual images). Encourage children to tell you about the images. This keeps a feeling of connection between you and will help you to pace the exercise. For example, when you say 'What does it (the cake) look like?' give children plenty of time to describe the sort of chocolate cake they are imagining. Show that you are imagining the same image by repeating back what you have heard them say or by making some appropriate sound (Mmmmmm!).

Think of a chocolate cake
Let's check out what your imagination is like today.

Sit comfortably and close your eyes. Imagine that you are in the kitchen. Imagine that it is your birthday and someone has made you a huge chocolate cake. It is in the fridge. You are allowed to go and get it.

Imagine yourself opening the fridge door. You see the cake on a big plate. What does it look like?… You take it out of the fridge. What does the plate feel like? How do you carry the cake? What can you smell? You put the plate with the cake on it onto a table. Someone comes and cuts a big slice for you. What does this person say while they are cutting the cake?

What happens to the cake as this person starts to cut it? You reach out to take the piece of cake. What does it feel like when you touch it? Then you take a big bite. What can you taste? Can you smell anything? What do you imagine yourself saying? Now let the images fade and, when you're ready, open your eyes.

See how good you are at imagining things!

Adaptations

- Substitute any food that is a favourite amongst the children with whom you are working.

- Simply ask the child to close his eyes and tell you about 'an orange' or 'a dog'; encourage expansion as appropriate ('Tell me a little bit more'; 'What does it feel like?' etc.).

Expansion ideas

- There are lots of different types of images. Some are like pictures, some are sounds (such as imagining a conversation or a tune in your head), some are feeling or sensation images (like imagining the feel of velvet or mud or imagining what it's like for your friend to feel sad).

- Sometimes we can experience a feeling such as sadness or anger or being happy just by imagining something. Can you think of a time when this has happened to you?

- Have you ever made up a story in your head? Have you imagined that you saw something that wasn't really there? Have you heard a noise and imagined that it was something scary? Have you ever remembered the taste or feel of something that isn't actually in front of you? Do you ever imagine that you are somewhere else or doing something different? These are all images and they come from your imagination.

- We all have the power of imagination and we can all use our imagination to help ourselves to sort out problems, feel good, cope with troubles when they come along and help us to do some of the things that we want to do.

2. Talking cats

Foundation elements, abilities and skills

☑ self and others (E)   ☑

☑ imagination – empathy (A)   ☑

☑ understanding questions (S)   ☑

The basic activity

Read the activity sheet *Talking cats (1)* (p.107), together, with plenty of pauses to allow the children to explore the image. Invite the children to draw or write about what they imagined.

Adaptations

- Use the prompt sheet *Talking cats (2)* (p.108).

- Imagine what it would like to be an ancient tree in a field or a new tree outside your house. What would it see and hear every day?

- Choose famous people and talk about what it would be like to be them. What sort of day would they have? Where would they live? What would they eat for breakfast? What would they wear?

- Invite the children to choose someone important in their life (parent, brother, sister, friend, grandparent, teacher, etc.) and write about what they think would be a typical day for them or draw some things that they would do, wear, eat, etc.

Expansion ideas

- If we do something regularly, we stop thinking about it too much after a while and just do it, but we can still imagine it or recall the pictures from our mind when we want to. In the same way, when something new is about to happen, we can imagine what it might be like.

- We can also imagine things that may never happen at all. Sometimes this is useful and sometimes we may make up things that worry us and we begin to believe that they are true.

2.1 Talking cats (I)

Imagine that you have a pet cat that can talk. This cat would like to know all the things that you do on school days. Make a list of (or draw) everything that you have to remember to do. Start your list with 'I wake up'.

You didn't have to wait until you had done each thing again before you wrote it did you? You just imagined what you do each day.

Time to stretch your imagination a bit further.

Imagine that your pet wants to tell humans what it's like to be a cat.

What would it tell you? What does it like to do? What does it hate doing? What is it good at? What would it most like to happen? What does it think is the best thing about being a cat?

Close your eyes so that you can really begin to str-e-tch your imagination while you imagine having a conversation with your cat.

2.2 Talking cats (2)

Imagine that you are a cat… Imagine that you can talk. You want to tell humans what it's like to be a cat. Here are some words you could use when you tell us. I'm sure you can think of a lot more.

Describing words (adjectives):

warm   furry   soft   happy   sleepy   tired

Doing words (verbs):

purr   stretch   jump   climb   run   chase   stroke
eat   drink

Naming words (nouns):

friend   basket   fish   milk

Close your eyes so that you can really begin to str-e-tch your imagination.

Imagine yourself being a cat… Imagine what that feels like…

Ask someone to write down what you say while you are imagining that you are a cat. Think of a good cat name and then start with that.

3. Memories

Foundation elements, abilities and skills

☑ self-knowledge (E)   ☑

☑ self-control (A)   ☑

☑ memory strategies (S)   ☑

The basic activity

Give children the following instructions, leaving plenty of pauses to allow them time to explore the images:

Close your eyes and imagine yourself being in your most favourite place. Imagine all the details of this place, the colours, shapes, sounds and smells that are around you. Spend a few minutes enjoying imagining that you are really there. What are you doing? What are you thinking about when you are in this place? When you are ready, open your eyes and draw what you imagined. Tell someone else about your drawing.

Adaptations

- Make up your 'ideal' holiday place and imagine yourself being there.
- Visualise walking around a farm or a zoo or a magic shop.
- Visualise a journey to another country.
- Imagine being a river. Where do you travel to? How do you move and change on different stages of your journey?
- Visualise what you would like to be doing at the weekend or in five years' time.

Expansion ideas

- Was it difficult or easy to remember somewhere familiar? Why was this?
- Was it harder or easier to imagine somewhere made up or somewhere that you know well? Why was this?
- Was it difficult or easy for you to think about what you might be doing at the week-end? What about in five years' time? Why was this?
- What helps you to remember places? What helps you to remember people?

- When you think about different places do you remember the sounds that you can hear there? What about smells? If you were at the seaside, what would you be able to hear, smell, see? What would the sand feel like under your feet if it was a hot day? What would the sand feel like if it was a cold, wet day?

- How can visualising something help us to communicate ideas and feelings to other people?

4. Storyline

Foundation elements, abilities and skills

☑ self-knowledge (E)   ☑
☑ effective listening (A)   ☑
☑ planning (S)   ☑

Children will need to do some research at home before this game can be played.

The basic activity

Players are given the task of researching their names in preparation for a subsequent session. Guide them with questions such as: Do you know what your name means? How was your name chosen? How important is your name to you? When you use your name, how do you use it? Do you like other people to use your full name or a shortened version, or do you have a favourite nickname?

Start by telling name stories in pairs. The children then take turns to introduce their partner to the group and say *one* thing they can remember about that person's name story.

Adaptations

- Research middle names.

- Construct fictional stories about how children were named (e.g. in the style of a legend, a fairy story or a news item).

- When working with an individual or in smaller groups, take time to hear each child's full name story.

Expansion ideas

- Was it easy or difficult to find out about your name? Did you learn anything about other people in your family that you didn't know already?

- Do you know anyone else with the same name as you? Are they anything like you or are they very different? Do you have a name that is a 'family' name, given to successive generations perhaps? What do you think about that?

- What did you find interesting about each other's name stories?

- Do you associate some names with particular characteristics? Why might this happen?

- Do you like to use a different name with your family and with your friends? If so, why?

5. Funny bones

Foundation elements, abilities and skills

☑ self-expression (E)   ☑

☑ adaptability (A)   ☑

☑ understanding/using verbs (S)   ☑

The basic activity
Use pipe cleaners to make moveable figures. Make up a funny story based on the different movements that you can make the figure do. Tell your story to two other people.

Adaptations

- The children make their own figure to keep or the facilitator makes several figures of different colours for children to choose from.

- Read *Funnybones* by Janet and Allan Ahlberg (Puffin re-issue edition, 2010) and retell the story using pipe cleaner figures.

- Make cardboard animal and people puppets that are secured at the joints with brass fasteners (split pins) for easy movement.

Expansion ideas

- Tell the story of the funniest thing that has ever happened to you.

- What sort of humour do you enjoy/what makes you laugh?

- Do you like telling jokes?

- When is it OK to laugh while someone is talking? When is it not OK?

6. Storybox trios

Foundation elements, abilities and skills

☑ self-confidence (E)   ☑

☑ mutuality – cooperation (A)   ☑

☑ sequencing ideas (S)   ☑

The basic activity

Collect miniatures or make objects from modelling clay/play dough. Put three related items into a small box (silk-covered sweet boxes or sparkly gift boxes are ideal). Children choose from a basket of boxes and make up a story about the three objects. The story can later be written up and displayed with the box.

Adaptations

- Distribute empty boxes to the children and ask them to choose three objects from a large basket of miniatures to put into their box. They then give this box to another child to make up a story.

- Children sit in groups of three and make up collaborative stories, taking one object each from the box.

- A cloth bag full of interesting objects is passed around the group. The first player takes an object without looking inside the bag and then starts off a story based on that object. The bag then passes to the next player who takes an object and must weave that into the story as quickly as possible. The story continues until all objects have been used.

- Themed objects are placed in a cloth bag (e.g. farm animals, a farmer and a tractor or small objects that might be taken on holiday). Each player takes three objects and makes up a whole story within a strict time limit.

- Volunteers tell stories based on one or more objects from the bag.

- Based on the ubiquitous feely bag idea, a number of related items can be grouped together in a see-through bag. Players try to guess the theme of the bag (e.g. beach holiday, zoo, space travel). They then make up a story based on the identified theme.

- Players remove one object from a themed cloth bag and hide it under a box in front of them so that no one else sees what it is. They then describe the object to the rest of the group (this can also be played in pairs). Everyone tries to guess the theme from this one object. The bag is then passed to the next person who does the same. Play continues until all the objects have been described even if the players have guessed the theme.

Expansion ideas

- Is it easier or harder for you to make up a story with objects or to make up a story with no prompts at all? Why is this?

- Do all stories have a beginning, a middle and an end?

- Could you use the same three objects that you had in your box to make up a completely different story? How many different story ideas can you think of using these three objects? For example, a sandal, a donkey and a straw hat could be used in a story about someone who goes on a donkey ride at the beach, a donkey that wants a straw hat but can only find discarded sandals, the adventures of a little boy who looks after the donkeys in a Spanish village, etc.

7. Shadow puppet stories

Foundation elements, abilities and skills

☑ self and others (E)   ☑

☑ adaptability (A)   ☑

☑ starting a conversation (S)   ☑

The basic activity

Each child makes a shadow puppet 'self' by tearing a piece of paper (tearing means that the shape has a 'fuzzy' outline and children don't feel the need to make it look too realistic). Attach the puppet outline to a straw or a pipe cleaner. Use an overhead projector to project the shadow puppet on to a blank wall. Make up a shadow story about two or more children meeting for the first time.

Adaptations

- Cut out animal shadow puppets. Make up a story about the animals that meet each other in a zoo for the first time.

- Make hand shadows and have a conversation between, for example, a rooster and a rabbit. For ideas about shadow puppets, try the Bill Douglas Centre for the History of Cinema and Popular Culture at www.exeter.ac.uk/bdc/young_bdc/shadows/shadows2.htm or try one of the many books on hand shadows such as *The Art of Hand Shadows* by Albert Almoznino (Dover Publications Inc).

- Make shadow puppet letters. Give the letters different characteristics and tell a story (e.g. 'Angry A' met 'Calm C'). What happened?

Expansion ideas

Puppetry is an excellent tool for promoting speech, language and communication skills. Here are just a couple of ideas related to shadows puppets:

- Talk about big/little; light/dark; changing shapes; casting shadows; increasing/decreasing; movement; theatre; plays.

- Look for your own shadows on the playground or on the pavement. Make your shadow jump, stretch, shake, curl up, etc.

8. Tell me my story

Foundation elements, abilities and skills

- ☑ self-acceptance (E)   ☑
- ☑ imagination – empathy (A)   ☑
- ☑ maintaining a topic (S)   ☑

The basic activity

Think up a title for a story which includes a player's name such as:

- Marcus the bold
- Amazing Craig
- Javed's dream day out
- Katie's greatest adventure

The child in question starts off the story. The rest of the group continues around the circle, saying one sentence each. This could be a completely imaginary story or could relate to something that everyone knows really happened.

Adaptations

- Players think up their own title for their stories.
- Players choose titles from a selection of three or four.

Expansion ideas

- Was this difficult, exciting, funny, easy?
- Did the group come up with some things that truly reflected each person's personality/likes and dislikes?
- How did it feel to listen to a story about yourself?

9. Scrambled

Foundation elements, abilities and skills

- ☑ self-confidence (E)   ☑
- ☑ imagination (A)   ☑
- ☑ sequencing ideas (S)   ☑

The basic activity

Take a well-known story (perhaps a favourite picture book) and summarise it in six easy sentences. Write these down or illustrate them in a simple way (or trace the outline of the original illustration for children to colour). Scramble them up and present them for children to sort them into the correct order.

Adaptations

- Children invent their own story in six parts, scramble them up and see if an adult can unscramble them. The child can tell you if you are right or wrong.
- Increase or decrease the number of parts.
- Retell simple sequences such as making a cheese sandwich.
- Retell a sequence backwards.

Expansion ideas

- Was this an easy or a difficult thing to do? Why was that?
- Can the story be told in a different sequence and still make sense?
- Could you make a cheese sandwich in a different order?
- What might help you to remember a sequence of events?
- Retell something that happened to you recently. Where does the story start? Where is the middle? Where does it end?

Some more ideas

Hot seating

- This encourages children to explore aspects of empathising with another person's point of view or feelings. The group listens to a short story or a description of an event. One child sits in the 'hotseat' in role as one of the characters from the story. The rest of the group are invited to ask this person questions in order to explore perceived feelings and situations from the character's perspective. Questions can be spontaneous or briefly planned beforehand.

Tunnel of thoughts

(Also known as *conscience alley* or *decision alley*)

- The group forms two lines facing each other. One person takes on the role of a character in a story that is faced with a decision or dilemma. This character walks down the centre of the tunnel as the rest of the group speak out thoughts in support of both sides of the decision (e.g. 'I should listen to this person because…', or 'I should walk away from this person because…'). The character, having consulted his 'conscience' in this way, has choice about what thoughts to take on board and what to discard. He then makes his decision on reaching the end of the tunnel.

Thought bubbling

(Also known as *thought tracking*)

- This is another way of encouraging empathic responses by exploring the 'private' thoughts of a character, usually at a point of crisis or dilemma in a story. One person takes on the role of the character and the rest of the group stand in a circle around him and take turns to 'speak the thought' that the character might be having at that particular point in the story. These thoughts might be different to or the same as the thoughts that the character is actually speaking.

  This can also be done in pairs, where two people take on the same character role and speak two different perspectives while the rest of the group ask questions about their actions and choices.

Paired improvisation

- Two people take on the roles of two different characters in a story and have a conversation for a pre-set period of time and with no prior planning.

Turn around theatre

(Suitable for 9–12 players per scenario)

- The success of this activity rests on the ability of group members to 'tune in' to each other and to work spontaneously as a team. The group is divided into three smaller subgroups who will act out the beginning, middle and end of a given scenario – for example,. 'You are with a group of friends walking home from school and you see a new member of your class being bullied by some older children'. The first subgroup is given a few minutes to sort out roles and then performs the first part of the play while the other groups watch. At an appropriate point the second group takes over and elaborates on the story. It is up to the third group to act out a suitable resolution to the situation.

- Retell well-known stories from a different point of view.

- Share traditional stories from different cultures.

- Invite children and guest adults to tell a familiar story in different languages. Talk about intonation and gesture and how these can help us to understand different parts of a story even if we don't understand the language we are hearing. Celebrate the diversity of languages.

- Make a story chain: take turns to say one word of a poem or one sentence of a story.

- Children stand in a line or circle and say one sentence each of a well-known story. Mix everyone up and try to retell the story, still keeping it in the right order (i.e. the children need to remember which sentence comes next). Or tell it in the wrong order according to where children are in the line/circle. One or more players try to reposition children in the right order, moving them around and asking them to say their sentence as often as needed until the whole sequence makes sense (although it may not be the same as the original story!).

- See also Chapter 13, *Parachute Games*.

Chapter 10

Conversation Games

General tips

- Breaking the social rules of conversations to produce strange or funny scenarios can be a fun way to reinforce conversation skills. Inject a great dollop of humour into games played in this section as often as you can!

1. Chinese whispers

Foundation elements, abilities and skills

- ☑ self-expression (E)   ☑
- ☑ effective listening (A)   ☑
- ☑ sentence construcion (S)   ☑

The basic activity

Players are seated in a circle. Player 1 whispers a word or short sentence to the next person in the circle, who whispers it to the next person and so on until it gets back to Player 1 again. The final word/sentence heard is then compared to the original version.

Adaptations

- Player 1 draws a simple shape or picture with one finger on the back of Player 2 who has to pass it on around the circle.

- Player 1 draws a simple picture on a piece of paper, then shows it briefly to Player 2 who has to draw it from memory before showing the new version to Player 3 and so on.

Expansion ideas

- Compare the different versions of the pictures or the spoken sentences. Is it easy or difficult to remember the details of what we see and hear?

- Talk about how things we say and do can be remembered inaccurately. What should we do if we think someone has misunderstood us or we don't really understand what someone else has said?

- When is it OK for something that you have said to be repeated to other people? When is it not OK?

2. Twenty questions

Foundation elements, abilities and skills

☑ self-confidence (E)   ☑

☑ perseverance (A)   ☑

☑ asking questions (S)   ☑

The basic activity

Everyone in the group writes the name of a famous person on a piece of paper (or these could be prepared beforehand by the facilitator). The papers are then shuffled and each person takes one without looking at it. This is taped to his back by the facilitator. Players form a circle and take turns to stand in the middle, turning around slowly so that everyone can read the label. The player in the centre can ask up to 20 questions to find out the identity of the famous person. The other players can only answer 'yes' or 'no'.

Adaptations

- Use animal pictures or characters from a book with which the players are all familiar.

- Allow more descriptive answers than just 'yes' or 'no'.

Expansion ideas

- How easy or difficult was it to think up questions?

- How did you use the answers to each question to help you to decide on the next question?

- In order to know someone well, we need to know lots of different things about them. What sort of things could we ask? Think about personality, opinions, likes and dislikes, etc.

3. Magic threes

Foundation elements, abilities and skills

☑ self-knowledge (E) ☑
☑ effective listening (A) ☑
☑ memory strategies (S) ☑

The basic activity

Players have three minutes to walk around the room and introduce themselves to three other people. Each player asks three people three questions. For younger children, this could be full name, something you hate and something you like. For older children, the questions could be your greatest achievement, your best birthday and your most treasured possession. Or one thing that makes you angry, one thing you do to 'chill out' and one thing you want to achieve.

When the time is up, everyone sits in a circle and recounts as much information about as many other players as possible.

Adaptations

- Pairs share the information and then introduce each other to the rest of the group.

- Players divide into groups of three or four and try to find three things that they all have in common. One person from each small group tells the whole group what these three things were.

- Pairs talk about something that they are wearing or what they most like to wear (e.g. a favourite jumper or favourite pair of shoes).

Expansion ideas

- What type of question is likely to produce a limited amount of information? What type of question encourages people to give more detailed information? How difficult or easy was it to remember what you heard? What would make it easier/harder to remember facts about other people? Why is it important to remember what people tell us about themselves? What does it feel like when someone remembers something important about you? What does it feel like when people get the facts wrong?

- Is it better to ask three questions all at once or to ask them one at a time? How long can you comfortably wait in order to give the other person time to think of their answer?

- What does it feel like to know that you have things in common with other people? Was it difficult or easy to find things in common?

4. Interviews

Foundation elements, abilities and skills

☑ self-acceptance (E)   ☑

☑ mutuality (A)   ☑

☑ giving personal information (S)   ☑

The basic activity

Drape a chair with a brightly coloured blanket or cloth. Players take turns to sit in the chair and are interviewed by the rest of the group. Questions can be about their likes and dislikes, wishes, holidays, favourite books, pet hates, etc., or they can be interviewed about a particular interest they have. There is an allocated time limit for each interview.

Adaptations

- Use two chairs, one for the person being interviewed and one for volunteer interviewers who can come and sit in the chair and ask one question before returning to their place in the audience.

- The interviewee takes on the role of a famous person or a character in a book.

- Use a microphone to add to the authenticity of the interview.

Expansion ideas

- How does it feel to have the chance to talk about yourself? How does 'being interviewed' compare to having a conversation with someone? Talk about taking turns in conversations and asking questions to show a genuine interest in the other person. What does it feel like when a friend asks you questions about yourself?

- How do you encourage someone to carry on talking or to give you more details about something?

- How do you show that you are thinking about what to say? What happens if someone asks a lot of questions without giving the interviewee time to answer?

5. Keep it going

Foundation elements, abilities and skills

☑ self-expression (E)   ☑

☑ effective observation (A)   ☑

☑ non-verbal communication (S)   ☑

The basic activity

Players sit or stand behind each other in a line. The first player taps the second player on the shoulder. This person turns to face the first player who then mimes a short sequence such as planting a seed in a pot and watering it, or cutting a slice of bread and spreading butter on it. The second player has to remember the sequence to show to the third player and so on. The final player tries to guess what the first player was actually miming.

Adaptations

- The sequence can be made longer and more complicated or simplified to include just two parts.

- Players work in pairs and pass on sequences of gestures which involve two people cooperating (e.g. folding a large sheet together).

Expansion ideas

- Did the sequence change as it was passed around the group? Why did this happen?

- Do you use gesture when you talk? Why is it helpful to notice people's body language?

6. Silent greetings

Foundation elements, abilities and skills

☑ self-awareness (E)   ☑

☑ adaptability (A)   ☑

☑ greetings (S)   ☑

This game requires plenty of space for players to move around freely.

The basic activity

Everyone walks slowly around the room, silently greeting each other in a friendly way – for example, a little wave, a long slow wave, offering 'high five', smiling, making eye contact, having a short 'conversation' between hands. The facilitator may need to demonstrate a few ideas first. There should be no physical contact during this. The aim is to see how many different ways players can greet each other successfully.

Adaptations

- Play a variety of music (e.g. culturally specific music, lively music, slow, gentle music) while players walk around the room and greet each other in ways that match the different rhythms and themes.

- Players meet and greet each other. After a short silent 'conversation' they say goodbye to each other non-verbally.

Expansion ideas

- Did you learn a new greeting or get a new idea and then try it out on someone else? Did some ways of greeting seem easier than others? What was the most fun/natural/relaxed way to greet others? Which one felt most like 'you'? Did you change your greetings to match other people or did pairs sometimes greet each other in completely different ways? How did that feel?

- What are some of the signs that you could look out for to show you that people are thinking about you or welcoming you into a group, even if they don't say anything (e.g. 'thumbs up', smile)? How might this help you if you are feeling anxious? Can you think of a time when you would be able to give this type of reassurance to someone else?

- How close do we stand to the other person when we greet each other?

- What are some of the other ways that people greet each other (e.g. shaking hands, a back slap, a hug)?
- What sort of things can you say to end a conversation? How do you know when a conversation is coming to an end?

7. Circle move

Foundation elements, abilities and skills

☑ self-awareness (E) ☑
☑ self-control (A) ☑
☑ non-verbal communication (S) ☑

The basic activity

Players sit in a circle. One person starts off a movement such as a shoulder shake. Each player copies this in turn until everyone is making the same movement. Then everyone stops in turn until the circle is still. The person sitting to the left of the first player then starts a different movement and sends this around the group in the same way. Do this as many times as feels comfortable, varying the speed.

Adaptations

- Two players sitting on opposite sides of the circle start off two different movements at the same time and send them in the same direction or in opposite directions.
- Players 'throw' the movement to each other across the circle by gaining eye contact with another player.

Expansion ideas

- Sometimes even small movements or changes in body posture can show other people how we are feeling or can add extra emphasis to what we are saying. How many emotions can you show just by moving your shoulders? What about when you move your forehead/eyebrows?

8. Just a minute

Foundation elements, abilities and skills

☑ self-reliance (E)   ☑

☑ perseverance (A)   ☑

☑ topic maintenance (S)   ☑

The basic activity

In pairs, children take turns to carry on a conversation for one minute without straying off the topic and without repeating themselves.

Adaptations

- Speaker 1 talks for 30 seconds about a particular topic. Other members of the group can challenge if they think the speaker has changed the topic. If the challenge is agreed, the challenger then becomes the next speaker.

- Pairs have a one-minute conversation where Speaker 1 is trying to maintain the topic and Speaker 2 is trying to change the topic.

Expansion ideas

- Was it easy or difficult for you to keep talking about the same topic? Why was this?

- Compare talking about something you are enthusiastic about and something that you know very little about.

- What are the differences between 'giving a talk' and having a conversation?

- Do you like to have pauses for thinking time when you have a conversation or do you like to have fast conversations?

Some more ideas

- Make a 'group' sentence, adding one word each.

- Play the good news and the bad news. Players sit in a circle. The facilitator starts off with a piece of 'good' news. The next person adds 'but the bad news is…' followed by the next player, who says but the good news is… – for example, 'The good news is that school is closed for the day… The bad news is that we all have extra homework to do' but 'the good news is that the homework is to write about the local funfair… The bad news is that the funfair is closed for repairs…' but 'The good news is that the owner of the funfair is giving away free ice cream… The bad news is they don't have any cones'.

- Talk about being creative in thinking up possible good news related to the bad news. Have you ever been in a difficult situation that turned out to be useful for you?

- How many questions can you ask about a given object?

- See also *Beginnings and endings (1)* and *(2)*, pp.58 and 76.

Chapter 11

Thinking Skills Activities

General tips

- It is important to remember that some children learn best with visual or auditory prompts, and that others need to physically engage in an activity.

- As with all areas of learning, children will tend to generalise speech, language and communication skills more readily if they have had plenty of opportunities to engage in problem-solving activities.

- In relation to problem-solving real-life interactions, the most common format is:

1. Identify the problem clearly and concisely.

2. Brainstorm as many solutions as possible, including any that might seem untenable.

3. Look at the consequences of each of the possibilities.

4. Choose the most useful strategies.

5. Try out one of the strategies.

6. Evaluate the outcome.

7. Keep, discard or alter the strategy in light of the evaluation.

I. Talking turns

Foundation elements, abilities and skills

☑ self and others (E) ☑

☑ mutuality (A) ☑

☑ reasoning (S) ☑

The basic activity

In pairs, players put one arm round each other and act as if they were one person. They talk about a given subject, with each person saying one word at a time to make sentences. This means that they have to guess what the other person is aiming to say, and it can get quite frustrating and difficult! Topics could include 'Why I like chocolate', 'What I did yesterday', 'My favourite holiday', 'What I learned at school this morning'.

Adaptation

- The audience asks questions and the pair has to answer one word at a time.

Expansion ideas

- Did pairs manage to cooperate to make sense even if they couldn't guess what their partner was going to say?

- Sometimes we think we know what other people are thinking. Sometimes we expect others to know what *we* are thinking!

2. The rule of the realm

Foundation elements, abilities and skills

☑ self and others (E) ☑

☑ effective observation (A) ☑

☑ problem solving (S) ☑

The basic activity

This game encourages players to work together in order to solve a puzzle about group rules.

Divide the group into two. Group A leaves the room. Group B makes up a 'talking rule' such as 'Every time you speak you must cross your arms' or 'Every time you finish speaking you must scratch your head'. The facilitator checks that everyone in Group B remembers to do this by asking each one a simple question such as 'Do you like chocolate' or 'How old are you?' Group A returns to the room and the facilitator repeats the previous questions or asks similar ones while group A observes. The aim is for group A to guess the rule. The emphasis is on group problem solving – if one person in group A guesses the correct rule, this means that the whole group has achieved. Older children can therefore be encouraged to confer before they guess the rule.

Adaptations

- Allow a maximum of five guesses.

- Rules for older and very able children can be quite complex such as 'When the facilitator asks you a question, it is the person on your left who answers' or 'You have to use the last word from the question to start your answer'.

- The whole group stays in the room and the facilitator chooses a place to set up his kingdom (e.g. the moon, the playground). Players say what they will bring if they are chosen to be part of the new kingdom. The rule that they have to discover relates either to the first letter of their own name or to the first letter of the place where the kingdom will be. The facilitator starts by giving a few examples such as 'Sandip would be welcome in the new kingdom if he brought snakes with him but not if he brought *money*. Miriam would be welcome if she brought *money*, but definitely not if she brought *jewels*'. The facilitator tells group members if they can join the kingdom or not according to what they offer to bring with them. This needs a strict time limit and therefore clues may need to be made more and more obvious to give everyone the chance to guess the rule and join the kingdom. Players should be encouraged to help each other out towards the end of the game in order to ensure that no one is left out.

Expansion ideas

- Do all groups need rules? Why/why not? Are some rules more useful than others?

- What does it feel like not to know a group rule when it seems as if everyone else knows it? What should groups do about that?

- Do different social groups have different rules? What are some of your school/ classroom rules? Why do schools have rules?

3. The minister's cat

Foundation elements, abilities and skills

☑ self-expression (E) ☑

☑ perseverance (A) ☑

☑ understanding and using adjectives (S) ☑

The basic activity

- Players sit or stand in a circle. The first person starts off by saying 'The minister's cat is an _____ cat (using an adjective beginning with A) and its name is _____ (giving it a name beginning with A)'. The next player then does the same for B and so on to the end of the alphabet. Traditionally, when someone fails to think of a suitable adjective they are out of the game, but this can be played in a non-competitive way too. Having a lead-in phrase reduces the complexity of the utterance and makes some of the answers ludicrously unlikely!

Adaptations

- This traditional speaking game draws on knowledge of the alphabet and the use of adjectives but it could be adapted for any number of themes – for example, verbs (the minister's cat likes acting) and adverbs (the minister's cat acts admirably); food (the minister's cat likes apricots) and so on.
- Play with just two people taking turns.
- Use a children's dictionary and a baby name book to look up suitable words.

Expansion ideas

- Are you better at thinking quickly or do you prefer to take your time with thinking?
- How would the game be different if you used a dictionary? Why?

4. Travelling bags

Foundation elements, abilities and skills

☑ self-reliance (E) ☑

☑ imagination (A) ☑

☑ memory strategies (S) ☑

The basic activity

Think of a variety of different activities or adventures that would need different equipment and clothing (e.g. mountaineering, deep sea diving, going to an adventure playground, visiting a hot country, visiting a cold country, going on a dinosaur hunt). Choose one of these at a time and play a round of 'I packed my suitcase and I took…' Each person has to remember what has already been packed and add one more item to the list. When the list gets too long to remember, choose another adventure and start again.

Adaptations

- Anyone can challenge an item that doesn't seem relevant for the particular adventure.
- Pack items beginning with a certain sound.
- Use mini suitcases made from tea bag boxes. Attach luggage labels to indicate destinations. Fill them full of pictures of clothes and equipment. Talk about how the contents link together.

Expansion ideas

- Was it easy or difficult to remember the items in the suitcase? Why was this?
- Compare this game to the traditional memory game where you can pack anything you like. Does it become easier or harder if the items are related? Why is this?
- What helps you to remember things?
- Is there anything that you think everyone ought to remember? Make a joint list.
- What is memory?

5. What's my line?

Foundation elements, abilities and skills

- ☑ self-expression (E)   ☑
- ☑ effective observation (A)   ☑
- ☑ deduction (S)   ☑

The basic activity

Each child takes a turn at miming an occupation for the others to guess. The others in the group can ask ten questions between them to help them to guess. Questions can only be answered by 'yes' or 'no'.

Adaptations

- Brainstorm a list of common occupations before starting the game.

- Use pictures representing occupations for children to choose from. These could all be kept in view so that the others can see they only have limited choices.

- Group members point to the picture representing the occupation being mimed.

- Play 'What's my game?' (e.g. snakes and ladders, noughts and crosses).

Expansion ideas

- What makes some occupations easier to mime than others?

- What can a person's gestures/body language tell us about how they feel?

- In what ways is miming different to/the same as speech?

- Why is miming useful? When might you need to use this skill?

- Are there any words/types of word that are difficult to mime? Are there any that are impossible to mime?

6. Invisible pass the parcel

Foundation elements, abilities and skills

- ☑ self-expression (E)   ☑
- ☑ imagination (A)   ☑
- ☑ categorisation (S)   ☑

The basic activity

The children are given a category to think about such as 'things you might find in a pencil case'. Everyone sits in a circle and passes an invisible parcel while the facilitator plays some music. When the music stops, the player who is holding the parcel pretends to unwrap it and takes out an invisible object from the chosen category which he has to mime to the rest of the group. Everyone tries to guess the object. Play continues as soon as someone has guessed. If no one guesses, then the parcel is passed around the group in the opposite direction.

Adaptations

- Use a real 'category' parcel with pictures in each layer of wrapping.

- Brainstorm a list of possible items first.

- Try miming different emotions at each layer.

Expansion ideas

- Was it easy or difficult to think of items to mime? Why was this?
- Did anyone mime an item that you were going to mime? How did that feel?
- Was it easy or difficult to guess what people were miming? Why was this?

7. Guess who!

Foundation elements, abilities and skills

- ☑ self-expression (E)   ☑
- ☑ adaptability (A)   ☑
- ☑ voice projection (S)   ☑

The basic activity

(This works best in a fairly large group where the players know each other well.)

A player is chosen as the first listener. He stands with his back to the other players. Three children take turns to disguise their voice and say a pre-chosen sentence such as 'Hi, it's great to see you'. Player 1 must try to guess the speaker's real identity. He is only allowed one guess for each voice. If he cannot guess correctly, the person who has managed to disguise his voice successfully takes over as listener. If he guesses all three voices correctly, he chooses the next person to be the listener.

Adaptations

- Increase the number of guesses allowed.
- Give time at the start for everyone to practise their disguised voice.
- Increase or decrease the length of the spoken sentence.

Expansion ideas

- Was it easy or difficult to disguise your voice? Why was this?
- What would the world be like if everyone sounded exactly the same?
- What makes voices sound different?
- Have you ever 'lost' your voice? Why/when might this happen?
- What did you do to disguise your voice? Can you change anything else about your voice (e.g. pitch, volume)?
- Do you like your voice? If you could swap it for another voice, what sort of voice would you swap it for?

8. If he/she were a musical instrument

Foundation elements, abilities and skills

- ☑ self-knowledge (E)   ☑
- ☑ imagination (A)   ☑
- ☑ understanding similes/metaphors (S)   ☑

The basic activity

Players sit in a circle. Player 1 leaves the room and the others choose someone in the group who will be described. Player 1 returns to the room and is allowed to ask ten questions in order to find out who the group have chosen. Each question must take the form of 'If this person were a _____ (musical instrument, house, car, bird, etc.) what kind of _____ would they be?' When Player 1 guesses correctly, another person leaves the room and the process is repeated.

Adaptations

- Instead of choosing a person, the group chooses an emotion for Player 1 to guess.
- Brainstorm as many different categories as possible that could be used for this game.
- Limit the categories to just two or three.

Expansion ideas

- We all have many different aspects to our personality. Sometimes the way that other people see us is different to how we see ourselves.
- How would you describe yourself to the group?
- How might your parents/brother/sister/teacher describe you? Would they be right?

Some more ideas

- Set the task of mastering a trick such as how to tie a knot in a piece of string without letting go of either end of the string (you have to start with your arms folded!). The children then have to explain to another group how to do it (without actually showing them) so that this second group can demonstrate it successfully. The whole group then works out what skills were needed in order both to solve the problem and to teach the trick to someone else.

- Try to work out the least number of questions you might need to ask in order to find out what animal a child is thinking of (they can only answer 'yes' or 'no'). What is the best type of question to ask? Try this out and see if your prediction was correct.

Chapter 12

Construction Activities

General tips

- Begin by using everyday objects that are already familiar to the child/children, but bring in a variety of new materials to supplement this.

- Give children plenty of opportunity to explore the materials and talk about them before you start the construction activity.

- Take children on a walk to collect construction materials – twigs, leaves, small stones, pine cones, moss, etc.

- Keep a large box full of cartons, cardboard tubes, etc. for children to choose from (painting these with bright poster paints beforehand can add to the fun and could be used as a separate activity for learning about shape and colour).

1. Make a model to show how the lungs work

Foundation elements, abilities and skills

☑ self-awareness (E)   ☑

☑ imagination (A)   ☑

☑ breath control (S)   ☑

The basic activity

Challenge children to construct a model of the lungs from a variety of materials such as bubble wrap, cardboard tubes, balloons, etc. Include some materials that probably won't be suitable. Invite children to demonstrate their models and talk about them.

Expansion ideas

- If you could improve the design of our lungs, what would you change? (You could use Bob Eberle's SCAMPER (see p.33) to look at ways that the design of the human lung might be altered.)
- What happens to our lungs when we talk? How does this compare to when we do physical exercise like running?

2. Towers

Foundation elements, abilities and skills

☑ self and others (E)   ☑

☑ self-control (A)   ☑

☑ problem solving (S)   ☑

The basic activity

Groups of children cooperate to build the highest tower possible with a selection of materials such as cardboard, drawing paper, masking tape and tissue paper.

Adaptations

- Children cooperate silently to complete the task.
- Build towers from dominoes or playing cards.

Expansion ideas

- What worked? What didn't work? Why was this?
- Is it easy or difficult to work silently as a group?
- How did you communicate with each other? Did everyone have the chance to contribute? Why? Why not?

3. Construct an obstacle course

Foundation elements, abilities and skills

☑ self-confidence (E)   ☑

☑ adaptability (A)   ☑

☑ understanding cause and effect (S)   ☑

The basic activity

Children construct a miniature obstacle course for a toy dog. The dog must be able to go through, under, over, between and around various obstacles. The children then demonstrate the use of the course for a 'judge' to say if it is suitable for dog trials (of course, it always will be!).

Adaptations

- Make a snail garden on a tray with obstacles for snails to climb up, down and into, go round, through and over. (Obviously, if you do put snails in this mini garden, tell the children that they must be released into a big garden later!)

- Use wooden curtain rings (remove the small screws), colourful gift boxes, slinky toys and socks with the toe cut off for a more unusual mini obstacle course.

- Older children can work together to design an obstacle course for a team-building exercise – overcoming each obstacle will require cooperation between potential players (can be done as a paper and pencil activity or as a model construction).

- Use a water tray to build an undersea world for divers to explore.

Expansion ideas

- Talk about obstacles and challenges.

- Do we always have obstacles to overcome in order to achieve a goal?

- Think of an obstacle that you have overcome. What helped you to overcome this? Did anyone else help you?

4. Construct a totem pole

Foundation elements, abilities and skills

☑ self-acceptance (E)   ☑

☑ imagination (A)   ☑

☑ categorisation (S)   ☑

The basic activity

Create a wooden totem pole with hooks and platforms that can be used for hanging objects on. Change the theme of the totem pole regularly and talk about all the different categories of objects. Include plenty of items with different textures and colours. For an animal theme, for example, include animal puppets, plastic animals and pictures of animals that have been drawn by the children.

Adaptations

- Encourage the children to suggest the theme for the week and to remember to bring an item for the next day/week.

- Make mini totem poles out of kitchen roll holders or the cardboard centres of kitchen rolls. Paint them with bright colours and use drawing pins or Blu-tack to attach small objects and pictures.

- Make clay totem poles with animals to represent personal qualities or personal achievements.

- Cut out a giant paper tree with lots of branches to hang on a blank wall. Tape different categories of objects onto different branches. Encourage children to find pictures of different objects throughout the week and to tape them onto the correct branch.

Expansion ideas

- What is a totem pole? How were they used?
- What strengths/skills/qualities do you have? How might these be represented on a totem pole?

5. Communication channels

Foundation elements, abilities and skills

☑ self-reliance (E)   ☑

☑ adaptability (A)   ☑

☑ initiating and ending interactions (S)   ☑

The basic activity

Using a box of art straws and masking tape, make something that you would use to send messages from an island or for communicating with outer space (set a time limit of ten minutes), then have that conversation.

Adaptation

• Combine everybody's structures and make a giant communication system.

Expansion ideas

• Where in your body would you put this piece of equipment to help you with communication? Where would you wear it?

• What would you need to think about if you were trying to communicate with aliens from outer space?

• Use activity sheets 5.1 and 5.2 for discussion and drawing.

5.1. Finding out a bit more

Let's imagine that you have contacted an alien with your communication system! Think of three things that you would want to ask.

1. _____

_____

_____

_____

2. _____

_____

3. _____

_____

Now imagine that you *are* the alien. You don't know anything about earth or the people who live here.

See if you can think of three things that you would ask.

1. _____

_____

2. _____

_____

3. _____

_____

5.2 Feelings

What do you think it would feel like to be an alien in a place that you didn't know?

Think of three words to describe how you would feel.

_____

_____

_____

What are some of the important things you would need to know?

_____

_____

_____

_____

_____

What else would help you to feel OK about being in a new place?

_____

_____

_____

Some more ideas

- Pairs or small groups use colourful saris and chairs (or bean poles held together with masking tape) to make a base/story den. They go into their den and decide on rules for their 'tribe'.

- Paint mini cereal packets in bright colours or cover them with coloured paper. Pin or glue them onto a large noticeboard. Cut out pictures from magazines that belong in different categories or begin with different sounds and post them into the marked boxes.

- Make jewellery with beads that have letters on to represent the sound that the child is currently working on – make necklaces, friendship bracelets, etc.

- Cooking together is a great way to encourage conversation. Make cakes and bread and share the end product. Make salt dough that can be used for modelling.

Chapter 13

Parachute Games

General tips

- With a little imagination, many games can be adapted to include the use of a parachute. Parachute games are fun for children of all ages and provide an excellent focus for outdoor play. You can be endlessly creative – a parachute can be the sea, the sky, a mountain, a lake, a caterpillar, a tent – anything that you want it to be!

- Although parachute games are normally played with groups, they can easily be adapted for two to three players by using a large piece of material such as a round tablecloth.

- As with any games involving the use of equipment, parachute games should be supervised by adults at all times. Small children can easily get themselves tangled up in a large parachute – at the very least this can be a scary experience; at worst it could lead to injury.

- Parachute games can be played with just two people or up to 40 with a full-sized chute.

- In order to maintain a good grip on the parachute, roll the edge up and tuck your fingers underneath the rolled fabric.

- Remind children to be careful not to bump into each other if the game involves swapping places. Do not allow them to use the parachute for tossing each other in the air.

1. Big ball parachute game

Foundation elements, abilities and skills

☑ self-awareness (E)   ☑

☑ mutuality (A)   ☑

☑ understanding and using opposites (S) ☑

The basic activity

Players hold the parachute at waist level and send a very large ball around the circle. One half of the players aims to try and keep the ball in the circle while the other half tries to send it out.

Adaptations

- Send several different-sized balls around the circle, either with everyone cooperating to try to keep the balls going in the same direction or with half the group trying to send the balls out of the circle.

- This game can be adapted for teaching and reinforcing a variety of opposites such as left/right; up/down; big/little; high/low; fast/slow; on/off.

Expansion ideas

- Was this easy or difficult? Why?

- Can you think of a project at school where everyone needed to cooperate?

- How does cooperation help with communication?

- How does communication help with cooperation?

2. Waves on the sea parachute game

Foundation elements, abilities and skills

☑ self-awareness (E)   ☑

☑ self-control (A)   ☑

☑ giving instructions (S)   ☑

The basic activity

Hold the parachute with both hands at waist level. Place a soft ball in the middle of the parachute. Take turns to give instructions for how calm or stormy the waves on the 'sea' should be, and you and the child/children move the parachute accordingly, while trying to stop the soft ball from falling off.

Finish with a calm rippling of the parachute and gently lay it on the ground. Sit quietly on the edge of the 'sea'.

Adaptations

- Tell the story of a storm brewing, from gentle rain to a tornado and then subsiding again. Players move the parachute according to the different stages of the storm.

- Players take turns to give instructions for moving the parachute in different ways at ground level (e.g. like ripples on a pond, like great waves, like a sheet of ice) while two or more players walk across the surface in an appropriate way to match the motion.

Expansion ideas

- Talk about speed of speech and the amount of emphasis we give to different words in a sentence (stress).

- Do you ever get so excited while you are talking that it is difficult to control your speaking?

- What does it feel like to use calm talking? What does it feel like to use fast talking?

3. Parachute name game

Foundation elements, abilities and skills

- ☑ self and others (E)   ☑
- ☑ self-control (A)   ☑
- ☑ remembering names (S)   ☑

The basic activity

Players crouch down around the outside of the parachute, holding tightly onto the edge. On a signal from the facilitator (or children take turns to say 'one, two, three, up'), everyone jumps up, making the parachute mushroom into the air. The facilitator quickly calls the names of two players who must swap places by running underneath the parachute before it floats back down.

Adaptation

- Players hold the parachute at waist level. A large soft ball is placed in the middle of the parachute. The facilitator says the name of each player in turn and everyone tries to send the ball across the circle to that person.
- Players are given names of animals, vehicles, fruit, etc.

Expansion ideas

- How easy or difficult is it for you to remember people's names?
- What helps you to remember names?
- Why are names important?
- Do you have a favourite name?

4. Blow up

Foundation elements, abilities and skills

- ☑ self-reliance (E)   ☑
- ☑ perseverance (A)   ☑
- ☑ breath control (S)   ☑

The basic activity

Make a mushroom with the parachute (see *Parachute name game* above). The idea is to try and keep the parachute inflated by everyone stepping under the parachute and blowing as hard as they can. This is not really possible for more than a few seconds but it is great fun while it lasts! Make sure everyone steps out from underneath the parachute quickly as it begins to float down.

Adaptations

- Try sucking instead of blowing!
- Hold the parachute at waist level and move in to the centre and out again in rhythm with breathing in and out.
- Say/sing different vowel sounds as you move the parachute up and down or move in and out.
- Increase/decrease volume on a hum or a vowel as you move the parachute.

Expansion ideas

- Talk about how our lungs work (see also *Make a model to show how the lungs work*, p.139).
- What happens if you change the speed with which you move the parachute? What happens if you change the speed of your breathing when you talk?

5. Story igloo

Foundation elements, abilities and skills

☑ self and others (E)   ☑

☑ mutuality – cooperation (A) ☑

☑ monitoring volume (S)   ☑

The basic activity

Lift the parachute up into a giant mushroom (see *Parachute name game*, p.150). Everyone quickly takes a step in and sits down onto the edge of the parachute so that it remains slightly inflated like an igloo. This is now a cosy place to tell stories, play circle games or just have a quiet conversation!

Adaptations

- Imagine you are going into a space ship and when you land (come out from under the parachute) you will be in a different world. What will you see? What will you hear?

- Use the parachute as a circular blanket. Everyone lies under the blanket with feet towards the centre and heads outside the parachute. Imagine that it is night-time and you are all on a camping trip in an exciting location. What can you hear?

Expansion ideas

- What is the most exciting story that you have ever heard?

- Where would you most like to go for a camping holiday?

- What is the best thing about being able to imagine something that isn't really happening?

6. Big bugs

Foundation elements, abilities and skills

☑ self-awareness (E)   ☑

☑ self-control (A)   ☑

☑ following instructions (S) ☑

The basic activity

Drape the parachute over a long line of players to make a big centipede or a Chinese dragon. One player stays outside to give directions, or holds the end of the parachute above his head so he can see where he is going, and leads the big bug around a large open space.

Adaptations

- Make trains and coaches with a driver at the front.

- Make submarines by having two lines of children under the parachute.

Expansion ideas

- Is it easy or difficult to move in a group?
- What does trust mean? Did you trust the caterpillar brain/train driver to give you the right instructions?

7. Wind-down activities

Foundation elements, abilities and skills

- ☑ self-reliance (E)   ☑
- ☑ self-control (A)   ☑
- ☑ attention control (S)   ☑

The basic activities

- Invite all the children to lie still under the parachute while facilitators gently waft it up and down over the top of them.
- Sit around the outside edge of the parachute and pass a smile or a hand squeeze around the circle.
- Invite the children to lie quietly on top of the parachute, listening to some gentle music or a short story.

Chapter 14

Music and Movement Activities

General tips

- Alternate between using CDs and unusual instruments such as home-made shakers, rain sticks or an ocean drum.

- Children who are not able to move or who have very restricted movements will still be able to enjoy movement activities if you attach a long soft scarf to your wrist and give them the other end to hold.

1. Vocal orchestra

Foundation elements, abilities and skills

- ☑ self and others (E)   ☑
- ☑ mutuality/cooperation (A)   ☑
- ☑ non-verbal communication (S)   ☑

The basic activity

The facilitator demonstrates how to 'conduct' an orchestra with hand movements that indicate, for example, loudly/softly, quickly/slowly, all join in, stop. Each person in the 'orchestra' sings a vowel or makes 's' or 'sh', etc.

Players stand in a row, in small groups or in a circle according to the size of the group. Conductors take turns to conduct the orchestra as a whole group and with duos, solos, etc.

Adaptation

- Divide the group up into smaller groups of four before starting. The smaller groups stand together and all make the same sound when the conductor points to them.

Expansion ideas

- What does it feel like to be the conductor?
- What does it feel like to be part of the orchestra?

2. Guess the voice

Foundation elements, abilities and skills

- ☑ self-expression (E)   ☑
- ☑ effective listening (A)   ☑
- ☑ control of voice (S)   ☑

The basic activity

Players stand or sit in a circle. Each player invents a unique vocal call – for example, a combination of vowels with different intonation patterns or a hum or a whistle. The whole group listens to each call in turn as the players say their first name and then their chosen sound.

One person stands in the centre of the circle with a blindfold on. The facilitator silently chooses someone to make their call. The person in the centre tries to name the caller. If she gets it right, she can have a second turn.

Each person has a maximum of two turns before the facilitator chooses another person to sit in the centre.

Adaptations

- Callers recite one line of a well-known song or a pre-chosen phrase that all the players are able to say/remember.

- The player in the centre asks 'Who is there?' and those in the circle take turns to answer 'me', making the guessing harder.

- Two people stand in the centre and can confer about the name of the caller.

- The person who was last in the centre can choose the next caller.

- Everyone changes seats before the caller is chosen.

- The players are split into pairs to practise their calls. One person from each pair then stands in the centre of the circle and is blindfolded. On a signal their partners make their chosen calls. The players who are blindfolded have to move carefully around the circle until they find their partner.

Expansion ideas

- How do we recognise individual voices? What makes our voices different? What might happen if we all sounded exactly the same? What words can we use to describe different voices (e.g. deep, gruff, loud, soft, like chocolate)? Keep these descriptions very general, rather than specific to individual players.

- Does your voice change according to how you are feeling?

3. Musical drawings

Foundation elements, abilities and skills

- ☑ self-awareness (E)   ☑
- ☑ imagination (A)   ☑
- ☑ understanding emotions (S) ☑

The basic activity

The facilitator plays a variety of music and the group draws whatever comes to mind while listening to the different rhythms and moods.

Adaptation

- Players bring in their own selection of music and talk about how they feel when they listen to it.

Expansion ideas

- How does music affect our moods? Is there a piece of music that always makes you feel sad or always makes you feel happy?

4. Puppets

Foundation elements, abilities and skills

☑ self-awareness (E) ☑

☑ self-control (A) ☑

☑ following instructions (S) ☑

The basic activity

Players pretend to be puppets. They start in a standing position with their feet firmly on the ground, their arms stretched upwards and fingers spread out as though they are being held up by strings. They imagine that the strings are very slowly being loosened so that their body starts to drop down. Start with just the fingers, then hands, arms, head and upper body, finally bending slightly at the knees. The same movements are then performed in reverse until all players are standing upright again with arms stretched as high as they can. Do this several times at varying speeds. End with a shake to relax legs and arms again.

Adaptations

- Contrast being a melting snowman with being a metal sculpture.

- Make the puppet movements in time to different types of music.

Expansion ideas

- What does it feel like to have a relaxed body? How does that compare to being tense?
- When are you most relaxed?
- What sorts of things help you to relax?
- What might make you feel tense?
- What can you do if you feel tense before you start to talk or while you are talking?

5. Feeling in control

Foundation elements, abilities and skills

- ☑ self-awareness (E)   ☑
- ☑ self-control (A)   ☑
- ☑ non-verbal communication (S)   ☑

The basic activity

In pairs, players take turns at being puppet and puppeteer. Without touching the puppet, the puppeteer pretends to pull strings to get different parts of the puppet to move in different directions and at different speeds. This works well if the puppet is lying down to start with and the puppeteer has to work out which strings to pull in order to get the puppet to stand up.

Adaptations

- The puppet is a lion and the puppeteer tries to make the lion climb onto a low platform and lie down.
- The puppeteer moves the puppet to show different emotions.

Expansion ideas

- How does your body move? What aspects of movements can you control (speed, direction, range)? Think about the complicated sequence of movements needed to stand up or sit down. How do we learn how to do this? Talk about how children make mistakes and fall over when they are learning, but as we get older we move without thinking about it. Can you tell when your muscles are relaxed and when they are tense? Do you ever think about your shoulders, your back, the backs of your knees?

- How did the puppet and the puppeteer cooperate? What did you each need to do? How easy or difficult was this? Which role did you enjoy the most?

6. Feeling good about being me

Foundation elements, abilities and skills

☑ self-reliance (E)   ☑

☑ perseverance (A)   ☑

☑ following instructions (S)   ☑

Read the exercise below to your child and see if you can both use your imagination to help you to stretch further than you thought you could.

Imagine that you are a cat. When cats have been sitting still for a while or when they have been asleep, they like to stretch out from their noses to their tails. See if you can stretch like a cat. Kneel down with your hands on the floor in front of you. Gradually begin to stretch your arms forward, walking your hands along the floor. Feel your body getting longer and longer… Now bring your hands back to just in front of you and start to stretch out your legs behind you instead. First one and then the other… Now lie on your back on the floor and stretch out your arms, spread your fingers as wide as they'll go… Stretch out your legs and point your toes towards the other side of the room… Now let everything relax again… Gently roll over onto your side and then very slowly sit up. Now curl yourself up into a ball, and when I say 'go', uncurl and stand up, reach up towards the ceiling as high as you can, really stretching your fingers upwards and standing on tiptoes. 'Go.' Well done! Now relax again and slowly curl up in a ball. I want to show you how clever your mind is. Instead of really stretching this time, I want you to imagine that you are uncurling and reaching for the ceiling. You can reach right up way above your head. You can touch the ceiling. You're so good at stretching you can go much further than you thought was possible. In your imagination, feel what it's like to stretch that far. See yourself doing it… Good. Now I want you to really uncurl and stretch up and see how far you go… When you imagined doing this, you told your body that it could stretch much further than the first time you did it…and it worked!

Now relax and then give yourself a little shake all over. Shake your arms and your hands. Shake your legs and your feet, shake your shoulders, shake your body.

7. Follow my walk

Foundation elements, abilities and skills

☑ self-acceptance (E)   ☑

☑ imagination/empathy (A)   ☑

☑ giving feedback (S)   ☑

The basic activity

Players stand in circle. A volunteer walks across the circle several times. The group members give positive comments about the way that the volunteer walked (e.g. 'You held your head up; you looked well balanced; you smiled; your shoulders were relaxed'). Then everyone tries to walk in exactly the same way to really feel what it is like to walk like this person.

Have as many volunteers as possible and reassure everyone that they will get a go at another time if they want to.

Adaptations

* Imagine a character role and try to walk as you think they would walk (e.g. the strongest person in the world, an old person, someone who has just been told some good news).

* Walk in different ways to reflect different emotions.

Expansion ideas

* Where do you generally look when you are walking in the countryside? What is your posture like? Why?

* Where do you generally look when you are walking in town? What is your posture like? Why?

* Where do you generally look when you are talking to a friend or when you are talking to someone that you don't know? Why is this?

* Talk about body language in different cultures.

8. If we were animals

Foundation elements, abilities and skills

    ☑ self-acceptance (E)   ☑

    ☑ adaptability (A)   ☑

    ☑ understanding and using adjectives (S)   ☑

This game requires a large space for players to be able to move around freely.

The basic activity

Take some time to brainstorm the characteristics that might be associated with different animals. For example, a cat could be calm, adventurous, agile and so on.

    Players silently choose an animal from the list that somehow shows something about their own character. Divide the group into two. Half the group imagines becoming their chosen animal for a short while – moving around the room, greeting other animals and finding out their 'character'. The other half of the group sits and watches. Those who are watching can get up at any time and tap an animal on the shoulder to guess its identity. If the guess is correct, that animal joins the observers. Keep going until all the animals have been guessed. The groups then swap over.

Adaptations

- The facilitator chooses one of the animals from the above game. Everyone in the group tries to act like that animal for 30 seconds. The person who originally chose the animal (in the first game) can give 'directions' (e.g. 'I'm a flamingo and I move like this. I speak like this. I don't like… but I do like… When I meet other flamingos I…'). There is no 'correct' way to explore being this animal – for example, it doesn't matter if the person giving directions says 'I'm a flamingo and I like to eat chocolate'! Everyone will need a turn at directing others in how to be their animal, so it is best to do this version of the game with small groups or in pairs.

- Everyone chooses a completely different animal, perhaps one with the opposite characteristic to the first one chosen. For example, if a player chose a noisy animal, she could try being a quiet one, fast/slow, big/small, etc.

- All players go back to being the original animals and stand or sit in a circle to introduce themselves to the group and say one good thing about being this animal (e.g. 'I am a leopard and I can run very fast'). Finish by 'stepping out' of the chosen animals. Everyone stretches and shakes their arms and legs and goes back to being themselves again.

Expansion ideas

- Are you sometimes like one animal and sometimes like another? Why is this?

- What does it feel like to behave in a different way to the way in which you would normally behave?

9. Feel it, do it

Foundation elements, abilities and skills

- ☑ self-awareness (E)   ☑

- ☑ self-control (A)   ☑

- ☑ expressing/recognising emotions (S)   ☑

The basic activity

Players stand in a circle facing each other. Volunteers take turns to take one step into the circle and show with their whole body the way they are feeling today. Then they say their name (also in a way that reflects the emotion) and step back. The whole group steps forward and reflects back the action and the original person's name. Everyone steps back. The next volunteer steps forward. Players do not need to name the emotions.

Adaptations

- Players start by crouching down low. Volunteers 'pop' up (like popcorn!) and then crouch down again when they have shown their feeling and said their name. The whole group pops up to reflect the feeling and then crouches down to wait for the next volunteer.

- The facilitator suggests a limited number of emotions such as happy, sad and angry. Volunteers pop up to show one of these emotions and everyone else guesses which emotion that person was showing.

Expansion ideas

- How many different emotions can you think of?

- Talk about degrees of emotion. Is excitement the same feeling as being pleased? Is furious the same as cross?

Appendix

Keeping it All Going: The Transfer and Maintenance of Skills

The following are just a few ideas for maintaining the learning that has occurred during the activities and discussions. The description of *Confidence Groups* comes from the second edition of *Helping Children to Build Self-Esteem* (Plummer 2007a).

Key points

- Transferring speech and language skills into progressively more complex and demanding situations needs to be done gradually so that children do not become disheartened.

- Children will be more motivated to achieve and maintain targets if these are *relevant*, *manageable* and *fun* and if the child feels *engaged* with the process (e.g. if he has helped to set his own targets or has contributed to the design of some of the activities and games).

In Chapter 4 we explored how play can provide a powerful learning experience for children at various stages of their development. For older children, discussions about what happened during a game or structured activity can greatly enhance the learning process, but, in some instances, further support may still be needed. The following suggestions draw on a range of cognitive and behavioural strategies to reinforce the appropriate use of skills in new or challenging situations. Above all else, the building and maintenance of speech, language and communication skills will be most effective when a partnership approach to learning is established. When children, carers, professionals and support staff work together to identify areas of need and existing strengths, then the carry-over from structured activities to more general usage is likely to be much more effective.

Modelling, shaping and reinforcement

We know that the shaping of some desired behaviours occurs quite naturally. Children learn from the models around them and will be rewarded in some form (perhaps by increased attention or direct verbal feedback) for correct responses. The strategy of recasting a child's utterances by including a target sound, word or structure is based on this idea (e.g. a child says 'tar' and the adult responds with 'yes – car').

Specific shaping, however, involves identifying the basic features of a skill and rewarding successive steps towards building that skill. This means that we have to be on the alert to spot actual moments of appropriate use of speech and language skills or indications of appropriate thinking in order to give realistic and specific feedback (see notes on praise in Chapter 4, pp.41–44). Such praise and feedback can do much to motivate children to persevere with their learning, but we should be aware that it can also be overdone and lose its potency. Realistic self-evaluation and self-reward should therefore also be encouraged so that there is a healthy balance between these two processes.

In order for both the intrinsic and extrinsic reinforcement of skills to have maximum effect, we also need to think about the relevance of particular skills for individual children. A child is much more likely to be motivated to learn and use his communication skills if he can see the personal benefits of doing so.

Setting realistic and relevant targets

Children need plenty of opportunities to practise the skills that they are developing, but such opportunities need to be carefully structured in order to avoid the risk of repeated failure because the target was perhaps too high or too vague. For instance, a child who has problems with attention control may need help in focusing on language with minimal distractions or, conversely, may need visual prompts such as picture cards to help him to stay focused. A child who has difficulty in imagining another person's point of view may need to start with tasks such as imagining what his bedroom would look like if it were painted a different colour, or what his day would be like if he were a giant or an animal, before he can imagine what it might be like for his classmate to be upset.

Setting realistic targets also means that we need to provide children with the opportunity to explore a range of skills and responses so that they have choices about which skills are most relevant for them to use for different situations. Children who are very reticent speakers – because of fear of stammering, for example – may need to take time to work towards asking questions in groups but may feel more comfortable practising questions in a one-to-one situation.

Mentors

Children can be allocated a 'mentee' for a specific period of time (an activity session, a day, a week). During this time they keep an eye out for their protégé and offer praise and encouragement, or support in other predefined ways. Children should have the chance to be both mentor and mentee. This also works well in families where a younger child can feel that he has something positive to contribute to another family member's learning. Because there is a time limit on this, there is also less chance of an individual stepping in too much and deskilling a child rather than supporting him.

Diaries, wikis and blogs

Older children who are learning IT skills may like to engage in setting up a blog (internet diary) where they can report on their own successes, or, better still, a group wiki which other members of the group can contribute to. A wiki allows children to make collaborative contributions and to ask each other questions, share experiences, etc. The children should know that this will be monitored by the group facilitator. It is a particularly helpful tool for the transfer and maintenance of skills when group members are unable to meet up between sessions.

Confidence Groups

Confidence Groups aim to emphasise and promote existing skills as well as developing new skills. They promote connectedness with peers in a very meaningful way – giving children a forum in which to be heard and accepted by their peers and giving them the opportunity to learn how to receive acceptance and 'positive regard' from others.

My own experience of using this format is that it has proved to be an invaluable tool – the children love doing it, and the respect and empathy generated between children has a marked effect in other situations. Their ability to self-monitor and self-evaluate in a realistic way is enhanced, and the positive feedback from peers is a major boost to self-esteem. Of course, once demonstrated and practised, the principles of focusing on foundation elements, abilities and skills, connecting with others in order to really 'receive' praise and respect, and the giving of positive, specific feedback can all be generalised for use in situations other than a planned Confidence Group.

The idea for these groups is based on the format for oekos groups, which are an established element of imagework training (for further information about imagework please see book by Dr Dina Glouberman or visit www.imagework. co.uk), combined with aspects of techniques developed by Lee Glickstein (1998) as a means of personal development in public speaking. Glickstein's work is well-known in the UK as a self-help tool for adults who stutter. Specialist speech and language therapists Carolyn Desforges and Louise Tonkinson from Nottingham have also developed a particular version of his approach which they use with children. With their kind permission I have taken some of the principles that they outline and have altered the format to create Confidence Groups.

Format for Confidence Groups

Where you are working with large numbers of children (e.g. a class), this works best if you split into smaller groups. I have facilitated Confidence Groups with up to 12 children participating, but obviously the size of the group depends partly on the length of time available and the number of facilitators/helpers who know the format.

Stage one

For these groups to work, there are three principles which need to be established with the children from the outset:

1. *Focus on the positive.*
When children take part in the group, whether giving or receiving feedback, they are reminded and encouraged to focus on skills not deficits.

2. *The group members offer support to the speaker.*
This is discussed with the children in terms of what 'support' means and how we show support and acceptance of others, particularly how we show acceptance non-verbally by fully listening.

3. *The speaker 'connects' with the audience.*
This is established by helping children to focus on eye contact and breathing calmly. Children are encouraged both to sense the acceptance from their audience and to be aware of physical ways in which this is shown. This may seem a difficult concept for some at first, but they can be reassured that there is no right or wrong way of doing this.

The children sit in a circle and are invited to relax and to 'tune into' themselves ('Notice what your body is feeling… Notice where your thoughts are drifting to… Be aware of the other people in the small group, then tune back into yourself again').

The first round in the group generally doesn't involve any speaking at all. Instead, the children each take a turn to walk up to the 'stage' (a pre-chosen space in the circle). They make slow eye contact with each of the group members in the audience and then walk back to their seat. The audience members return eye contact and silently 'send' their complete acceptance. The 'speaker' is asked to be open to receive this acceptance. When the child has returned to his seat, specific, truthful feedback is given by the group facilitators on looking confident, walking in a confident way, using calm breathing to settle himself, gaining support by using eye contact, etc. The same format can be used with the children remaining seated and taking turns around the circle if this is more appropriate.

Stage two

The children take turns to walk up to the speaker position. They give and receive natural, gentle eye contact to everyone in turn and can then choose whether or not to say one word or a short sentence. They could perhaps introduce themselves or say something that they like, or just say 'hello', before returning to their chairs. This time feedback is given primarily from group members with a small amount of feedback from facilitators. The facilitators then praise the group members for the content and quality of the positive feedback given.

Stage three

The children walk up to the speaker position, take time to settle themselves, look around the audience and then say one or two sentences appropriate to the theme for the day. Once again, the other members of the group simply listen. The speaker is then given feedback by facilitators and group members on particular skills as appropriate. For example, the theme might be 'Things I have enjoyed do-ing' or 'What I did yesterday'; a particular speech and language target might be 'using the past tense' and the speaker might say something like 'I swimmed two lengths of the swimming pool'. Children are encouraged to give very specific, positive feedback about *what the speaker has just done* such as 'You smiled when you told us that and you looked as though you felt really good about your success', 'You were very brave to go first and speak in front of the whole group' or 'You kept really good eye contact when you said that'.

Of course, this sort of descriptive feedback will come from adult facilitators to start with in order to give an appropriate model, but if you encourage this as a regular feature of groups, children will quickly recognise all the different things they can praise. Facilitators might also include comments such as 'When you told us that you swam two lengths, you looked really proud of yourself' in order to model the correct target, in this instance the correct form of the verb..

Facilitators continue to praise group members for their positive feedback ('You picked up on a very important point in your feedback' or 'You are really noticing how people show their feelings', etc).

Stage four

Gradually increase the time for each person to speak when this feels right, but maximum time should be around two minutes. Keep an eye on the time to ensure that everyone gets an equal go.

Activities Index

References

Ainsworth, M.D.S., Bell, S.M.V. and Stayton, D.J. (1971) 'Individual Differences in Strange Situation Behaviour of One-Year-Olds.' In H.R. Schaffer (ed.) *The Origins of Human Social Relations*. London: Academic Press.

Ainsworth, M.D.S., Blehar, M.C., Waters, E. and Wall, S. (1978) *Patterns of Attachment: A Psychological Study of the Strange Situation*. Hillsdale, NJ: Lawrence Erlbaum.

Allen, R. and Wasserman, G.A. (1985) 'Origins of language delay in abused infants.' *Child Abuse and Neglect 9*, 3, 335–40.

Bandura, A. (1977) 'Self-efficacy: Toward a unifying theory of behavioral change.' *Psychological Review 84*, 2, 191–215.

Bandura, A. (1989) 'Perceived self-efficacy in the exercise of personal agency.' *The Psychologist: Bulletin of the British Psychological Society 2*, 411–24.

Botting, N. and Conti-Ramsden, G. (2000) 'Social and behavioural difficulties in children with language impairment.' *Child Language Teaching and Therapy 16*, 2, 105–120.

Boyle, J., McCartney, E., O'Hare, A. and Forbes, J. (2009) 'Direct versus indirect and individual versus group modes of language therapy for children with primary language impairment: Principal outcomes from a randomized controlled trial and economic evaluation.' *International Journal of Language and Communication Disorders 44*, 6, 826–46.

Bryan, K. (2004) 'Preliminary study of the prevalence of speech and language difficulties in young offenders.' *International Journal of Language and Communication Disorders 39*, 3, 391–400.

Cohen, D. (1993) *The Development of Play* (2nd edition). London: Routledge.

Conti-Ramsden, G. and Botting, N. (2004) 'Social difficulties and victimization in children with SLI at 11 years of age.' *Journal of Speech, Language, and Hearing Research 47*, 145–161.

Cooper, M.L., Shaver, P.R. and Collins, N.L. (1998) 'Attachment styles, emotion regulation, and adjustment in adolescence.' *Journal of Personality and Social Psychology Volume 74*, 5, 1380–97.

Dalton, P. (1994) *Counselling People with Communication Problems*. London: Sage.

Davies, K., Lewis, J., Byatt, J., Purvis, E. and Cole, B. (2004) 'An evaluation of the literacy demands of general offending programmes.' *Home Office Findings 233*. London: Home Office.

Durham, C. (2006) *Chasing Ideas: The Fun of Freeing Your Child's Imagination*. London: Jessica Kingsley Publishers.

Dwivedi, K.N. (1993) 'Play, Activities, Exercises and Games' in K.N. Dwivedi (ed) *Group Work with Children and Adolescents. A Handbook*. London: Jessica Kingsley Publishers.

Eberle, B. (2008) *Scamper On: More Creative Games and Activities for Imagination Development*. Waco, TX: Prufrock Press.

Garmezy, N. (1996) 'Reflections and commentary on risk, resilience, and development.' In R.J. Haggerty, L.R. Sherrod, N. Garmezy and M. Rutter (eds) *Stress, Risk, and Resilience in Children and Adolescents: Processes, Mechanisms, and Interventions*. Cambridge: Cambridge University Press.

Garvey, C. (1990) *Play*. London: Cambridge, MA: Harvard University Press.

Gerhardt, S. (2004) *Why Love Matters: How Affection Shapes a Baby's Brain*. London: Routledge.

Glickstein, L. (1998) *Be Heard Now! Tap into Your Inner Speaker and Communicate with Ease*. New York: Broadway Books.

Goleman, D. (1996) *Emotional Intelligence: Why it Can Matter More than IQ*. London: Bloomsbury.

Gore, S. and Eckenrode, J. (1996) 'Context and process in research on risk and resilience.' In R.J. Haggerty, L.R. Sherrod, N. Garmezy and M. Rutter (eds) *Stress, Risk, and Resilience in Children and Adolescents: Processes, Mechanisms, and Interventions*. Cambridge: Cambridge University Press.

Harter, S. (1999) *The Construction of the Self*. New York: Guilford Press.

Jerome, A.C., Fujiki, M., Brinton, B. and James, S.L. (2002) 'Self-esteem in children with specific language impairment.' *Journal of Speech, Language, and Hearing Research 45*, 700–714.

Leventhal, H., Brisette, I. and Leventhal, E.A. (2003) 'The common-sense of self-regulation of health and illness.' In L.D. Cameron and H. Leventhal (eds) *The Self-Regulation of Health and Illness Behaviour*. London: Routledge.

Miller, W. R. and Rollnick, S. (2002) *Motivational Interviewing*. New York: The Guilford Press.

Osborn, A.F. (1993) *Applied Imagination: Principles and Procedures of Creative Problem-Solving* (3rd Edition). Creative Education Foundation (original edition 1953).

Paley, V.G. (1991) *The Boy Who Would Be a Helicopter*. Cambridge, MA: Harvard University Press.

Pless, I.B. and Stein, E.K. (1994) 'Intervention research: Lessons from research on children with chronic disorders.' In R.J. Haggerty, L.R. Sherrod, N. Garmezy and M. Rutter (eds) *Stress, Risk, and Resilience in Children and Adolescents: Processes, Mechanisms, and Interventions*. Cambridge: Cambridge University Press.

Plummer, D. (2007a) *Helping Children to Build Self-Esteem*. (2nd edition) London: Jessica Kingsley Publishers.

Plummer, D. (2007b) *Self-Esteem Games for Children*. London: Jessica Kingsley Publishers.

Plummer, D. (2008a) *Anger Management Games for Children*. London: Jessica Kingsley Publishers.

Plummer, D. (2008b) *Social Skills Games for Children*. London: Jessica Kingsley Publishers.

Robertson, S. and Weismer, S. (1999) 'Effects of treatment on linguistic and social skills in toddlers with delayed language development.' *Journal of Speech, Language, and Hearing Research 42*, 5, 1234–48.

Rogers, C. (1961) *On Becoming a Person: A Therapist's View of Psychotherapy*. London: Constable.

Rutter, M. (1996) 'Stress research: Accomplishments and tasks ahead.' In R.J. Haggerty, L.R. Sherrod, N. Garmezy and M. Rutter (eds) *Stress, Risk, and Resilience in Children and Adolescents: Processes, Mechanisms, and Interventions*. Cambridge: Cambridge University Press.

Snowling, M., Bishop, D.V.M. and Stothard, S.E. (2000) 'Is preschool language impairment a risk factor for dyslexia in adolescence?' *Journal of Child Psychology and Psychiatry 41*, 5, 587–600.

Sunderland, M. (2006) *The Science of Parenting*. London: Dorling Kindersley.